IS THIS AN ILLNESS OR AN ACCIDENT?

01 02 03 04 05 29 28 27 26 25

Caitlin Press Inc.
3375 Ponderosa Way
Qualicum Beach, BC V9K 2J8
www.caitlinpress.com

Text design by Vici Johnstone
Cover design by Azlen Elza
Cover photo by Weston Fuller
Printed in Canada

Caitlin Press Inc. acknowledges financial support from the Government of Canada and the Canada Council for the Arts, and the Province of British Columbia through the British Columbia Arts Council and the Book Publisher's Tax Credit.

Canada Council for the Arts | Conseil des Arts du Canada | British Columbia Arts Council | Funded by the Government of Canada | Canada

Title: Is this an illness or an accident? / by Daniela Elza.
Names: Elza, Daniela, author
Identifiers: Canadiana 20240474066 | ISBN 9781773861630 (softcover)
Subjects: LCSH: Elza, Daniela. | LCSH: Belonging (Social psychology) | LCSH: Home—Psychological aspects. | LCSH: Identity (Philosophical concept) | LCGFT: Essays.
Classification: LCC PS8609.L93 I7 2025 | DDC C814/.6—dc23

Is This an Illness or an Accident?

essays

Daniela Elza

Caitlin Press 2025

Language spits out bodies
at the wrack line of receding glaciers,
words become flesh in the ashes of forest fires—
shaped by matter, language is shaping matter.

—Ian Thomas, *Green Islands*

To those who are curious.
To all who have walked by my side,
shared a word, a laugh.

Table of Contents

But Where Are You *Really* From?

It is eight in the morning in July and the sun crawls into bed with me. Its gaze meets the bevelled edges of the mirror and throws rainbows across the room. A blinding beam steals onto my pillow and elbows me out of bed. This is the first room I remember in Sofia, Bulgaria. Thirty-five years ago, I woke up to a different alarm in this room—a German clock that seemed to run forever on a single battery. I only remember changing the battery twice. I retired it when my kids complained its tick-tocks kept them awake—a sound I was used to falling asleep to in my grandmother's house. At that time, there were two beds, two desks and imaginary lines delineating my side of the room from my sister's side. These lines shifted, were often contested and required constant renegotiations.

My son and I are visiting my parents. This is the continent I was born on. It is not the continent I grew up on. Neither is it the continent I live on now. I am a third culture kid. The last time they saw their grandson was a decade ago, when he was five years old. Once they stop talking about how tall he is or who he looks like the most, they're going to have to get to know him all over again.

Of course, I couldn't wait to go to the book bazaar downtown. You can find anything between two covers there. I ask one of the sellers for an out-of-print book on metaphor. She likes a challenge; she'll find it. She talks to me as though I'm not from here.

"How do you know?" I ask.

"I know," she says, with a smile and a firm tilt of her head to underscore her certainty.

I'm startled when people treat me like a foreigner in Sofia. I was born here, have lived and studied here. Do I speak Bulgarian too carefully? Perhaps I speak *too proper*? I sift words between the two languages as if they are some precious cargo. I am Bulgarian but not Bulgarian enough.

My parents are bound by cultural norms and beliefs they expect me to abide by. I did not know that my dad would be insulted when I dropped my middle name (his first name) when I got married. I assumed the family name was more important to keep. Most of my early life, I heard my grandmother lament that, with two girls in the family, there would be no one to carry the family name forward. When a woman marries in Bulgaria, she is marked as her father's daughter (middle name) and as her husband's wife (last name). It was too late when I found out. I also did not know the unspoken rules of how to name the first boy born in the family, which caused me some grief years later. There's much they have not passed on in their determination to help me fit in somewhere else. They forget my heritage spans continents. Patriotism and nationalism are threadbare words to me. There are no clear lines here either. It means I will often be misunderstood. Regardless of whether we speak English or Bulgarian, or some version in between, our words still clash with unspoken expectations. We are left hanging on them, wondering what we should have said instead.

I grew up in Maiduguri, Borno State, in the north of Nigeria, but I am not Nigerian enough. I've lived on the North American continent for over thirty years now. I'm still not "American" enough. The three places I have called home have expectations of me I cannot fully fulfil. This shifting of home has become home. How many shadows my body throws depends on how many lights are turned on me, who is asking the questions, how bright their interrogation. Some days, it is exhausting to be so *multiple*. It is hard to feel both from here and not from here. On other days, it feels like a blessing. The different languages and cultures I span serve me like a pocketful of prisms through which I can refract any number of ideas, problems and encounters. This enriches my every day. Every day is an adventure.

On the way to Sofia, we stop in Venice. It's our first time here. I finally meet poet Arlene Ang in person. We have been writing poems-between-two, line by line, across cultures and borders since 2010. Here, we meet face to face. Serendipitously, the place we are staying happens to be walking distance from her house. We go to the old city. We jostle through throngs of tourists. Over a few days, we rub off a dozen hours of our soles on Venice stones. I feel less foreign here. We all stand out. We move like a stream of consciousness, a sentence that might eventually make sense. We take narrower side streets, avoid the crowds. Over the Crooked Bridge, past the Priest's Lane, we discover an alley about three feet wide. Dozens of doorbells suggest this dead end is also home to some. A man in flip-flops weaves alongside us for a few blocks, then ducks into a door. A glimpse of a woman and child inside. Was he going home? Does his sense of belonging change under this tourist occupation?

The newly built Calatrava Bridge (ponte della Costituzione) arcs over the Grand Canal. We climb up its arched back. Just when you think you have seen the sights, the buildings, the sky and the water transform with the light, tiptoeing into twilight. We are stolen by the view. As we begin our descent on the other side of the bridge, it's hard to see where the oddly spaced steps begin. The last thing you think of here is watching your step. I trip on the first step, tumble as if to prove a point. I later find out the bridge has had many victims, which gave it its nickname: the Bridge of the Fallen.

This bridge is like those unspoken expectations people have of me. The pitfalls usually arc away, are oddly spaced, and hard to see. I cannot fully relax in the crossing. The cultural steps I trip on are invisible until I fall.

I could be as much Nigerian as I am Bulgarian but no one ever asks. I don't look Nigerian. "You have an accent," someone diagnoses. That comment automatically places me in the you-are-not-from-here category and betrays the speaker is not aware they, too, have an accent. For a year in England, and for six years in Athens, Ohio, I was bombarded with the question, *Where are you from?* It felt like a question asked for the purpose of pigeonholing me into something the speaker knows. In the United States, I'm an alien. But they still asked where I am from. Aliens come from outer space. I was tired of coming up with new planets. No place on Earth was good enough for my origin. No wonder I never felt at home there; no wonder they have so many alien sightings.

Home is not just something I embrace but also what embraces me back. In Canada, I am mostly asked if I am from Montreal. I find it surprisingly comforting to finally be in a place where people locate me in the same country as themselves. As an immigrant here, I feel comforted that *from-somewhere-else* is not my primary and most identifying feature. When someone asks me now, *But where are you really from?*, I ask, *How much time do you have?* This essay is not enough but it's a beginning.

We are clearly foreigners in Venice. We don't speak Italian.

We repeat names and only approximately. We take too many photos. We ask too many questions. When locals answer in Italian, or a mix of English and Italian, I don't know if they're answering the question I asked. The cicadas mesmerize us; the heat makes everything evaporate. I count the days till we land in Sofia.

I feel at home in Sofia. Vitosha mountain rises above the city, claims the view. It's the ever-present presence. I've dreamt with this mountain. In the morning, it's a hazy outline; by noon, it's three dimensional. The last snow patch slowly melts and is almost gone into the summer heat. My mother tells me: *When that white dot of snow disappears, it's time to go to the beach*. This kind of thinking is familiar. When they say you don't eat fish (риба, pronounced *ree-ba*) in months that don't have the letter *r* in them, I know what they mean. Between *ashes on your tongue* and *from your mouth into God's ear*, the mountain turns shades of purple against the sunset sky. Familiar thoughts, like comfort food, are easier to fall asleep to. Feeling at home is easier than feeling I belong. Belonging seems to be something I have to earn.

Today, we walk for hours on the path that circumnavigates the base of Vitosha, a green tunnel that narrows and widens, a one-hundred-kilometre path with an occasional view of the sprawling city—the place from which we view the mountain each day. This path doesn't ask where I came from nor where I'm going. It doesn't question me. I'm here each moment anew. This is not just refreshing; it captures my imagination. We are already busy enough navigating each other's complex maps. The words we put on these maps move around, betray our expectations and our arrival. I never know which shadow will come forward to prove I exist in my multiple iterations. Figures of speech, figures of mourning, my shadow blasted against cultural walls. Here in the woods under the gaze of the creaky pines and birches, the rushing mountain river, I barely throw a shadow, except the one the sun gifts me from time to time. I don't have to question that I come from this place, this earth, these trees. Botanist Diana Beresford-Kroeger scientifically demonstrates something we know deep in our bones—trees have the same chemicals we have in our brains, they have the neural ability to listen and think, they have all the component parts necessary for a mind or consciousness.[1] In other words, a forest can think. I can feel that. We take turns communicating with each other. We take turns breathing each other in. I am the water that whirlpools, stands still, then leaps, rushing down the hill.

In the National Museum of Natural History in Sofia, within a few hours we walk through millennia, across fourteen centuries of Bulgarian history. We wander from room to room like words attempting to fit themselves into the long sentences of the past. This time, the five centuries of Ottoman occupation seemed toned down and subdued, as though we had missed a room. I wandered back to see if we indeed had skipped one of the display rooms. Had five centuries of bloody history evaporated? How to make sense of that? Is it because of the rising tensions in the world again? These tensions have not stopped rising since. Wars are now fought on multiple fronts. In Canada, we recently "celebrated" 157 years. If we acknowledged the First Nations, Métis and Inuit in this history, when would history begin in our history books? We live on stolen land. Each of us an immigrant arriving in a once-upon-a-time story with our own once-upon-a-times—stories also full of beginnings, crowded with shadows to be reckoned with. When we brought the government down in Bulgaria, there were no history books in the schools the next year. The ministry of education at the time issued a pamphlet to guide teachers that year. Who will be writing the next history textbook?

In Primorsko, we wake up early to see the sun rise out of the Black Sea. A path through a grove of oaks and dunes leads us to the beach. My dad and mom walk with purpose, like turtles, home in on the vibrations of the sea and the morning light. There is no stopping them. My son and I, bleary-eyed, follow to catch up. My son takes a photo of me with my arms raised; the morning sun looks like it is nestled in my palms, as if I am plucking the light right out of the sky.

We swim in the warm water and float atop the mischievous waves. They slap the shore with such a passion, knock us off our feet. In their powerful, tireless sweep, the sands beneath shift, the terrain and depth change daily. The past, too, tosses and whirls us, drags us in its tow. We go in together. Play. Nothing to hold onto here but each other.

Our flight back has a layover in Munich. We meet in person with Dorothee, a woman I had only met virtually around an online publication years ago. We take the train to the old city and climb out of the metro into early morning chanting—a pilgrimage of the Pious Brothers. My German is so bad that I could not tell what they were protesting or demanding. We, too, are on a pilgrimage but ours is harder to name. Construction and delivery trucks add to the din.

At home in Vancouver, the air is thick with smoke and ash blowing in from the raging fires. We live on orange light, under a dim red sun. The news gives little hope. Trump is elected president and hope goes missing for months. The mountains are obliterated for days. The place looks unfamiliar and foreign. We walk around in a physical and mental haze; like partial eclipses, we throw unfamiliar shadows. My body knows something my mind is trying to catch up to, grieves. Some panic, some take it as manifestations of prophecy. More often than not, it seems to shake us awake to the predicaments we have gotten ourselves into and with which we now have to reckon. Suddenly, we are fragile, talk to one another more. How little it takes to throw us off, how quick to be unsettled. I think of that man in the flip-flops in Venice.

When the pandemic hit hard, my school moved to online teaching. After eighteen weeks of talking to my students though a screen, I was not sure if my voice would recover or come back to "normal." Nothing has come back to normal since. I look at the photo we took on the edge of the Black Sea, with the rising sun between my palms. Today, it feels more as if I am pushing the light up for myself and others.

All my life, belonging has been a two-way street in a volatile neighbourhood, subject to changes without notice. I may want to belong, but if I am not accepted, I am constantly reminded I do not belong. I am at the mercy of optical illusions in this kaleidoscope of a city. I'm the tourist who also gives directions in an emotional country I have to negotiate and map every day. With the impossible rents, it's hard to house the many traits and features assigned to me. They make dissonant roommates and I'm exhausted with the negotiations of the house rules. After my separation from a twenty-year marriage, I had to again renegotiate home. Some days, I have to be enough of a home to come home to.

A ray of light shines through with the preparations to welcome a Syrian family in one of the units in our housing co-operative. After so many beginnings, I cannot imagine starting from scratch again. Beginnings still hold a special place for me but moving to new places has become tiresome. We make them a pie, introduce ourselves, learn one another's names. I feel Canadian enough when I am accepted as one. I feel more Canadian when I can welcome others here. And that is a pretty good place to begin.

Be a Link, Not a Fragment

Above the dining room table in my grandmother's kitchen hung a photo of my grandfather in military uniform. She kept his medals enshrined in an old gift box, but mostly she spoke of how handsome he was when they met and how he'd write *I love you* on the bottom of her shoes each time he left the house. To this day, I'm not sure if that was an expression of his love or jealousy. He was my only living grandfather. We often took rides in his Volga to birch woods drenched in sun. He told me stories of encounters with wolves and of bloody blades as we strolled among trees he helped plant as a young soldier. Sometimes, he spoke of his war years—from lieutenant to captain to major. Nothing grand. He sat in damp trenches, ate his lunch next to a pile of dead bodies—his friends, his comrades. They had to keep the rats away and sometimes eat them.

"So cold," he said. "At night, I'd sit in a pile of hay up to my neck and read Plato."

Whenever I asked my grandmother about her life, she'd wave her hand past her ear as if shooing a bug away and utter the dreaded words: *Don't look back*. History was my least favourite subject in school, not just because it was reduced to mostly dates and names. Bulgarian history is very bloody. Stylized images of churches full of massacred people were terrifying for the young impressionable me and to this day are lodged in my mind. You can easily grow resentment and hate for people you've never met.

Bulgaria suffered a lot from the Ottoman Empire and from most invasions before and after. Its people won many battles on the ground but the government was often on the wrong side of the war. I used to comfort myself with: *Know your history or it will repeat itself*. Today, we see history repeating itself and we are all terrified with what is rearing its ugly head.

War was a spectre that ate at our table. My grandmother lived through both world wars. Were her stories as dramatic as the history books claimed? She'd speak of the rationing and what they couldn't afford to buy. She used that strategically to make us finish the food on our plates. But she spoke little of wartime.

My grandfather survived the war, passed his philosophy exam and graduated. He even survived my grandmother's scorn. The Volga, with its plush red seats, never lost its smoky whiff, even when he stopped smoking after a heart attack. Eventually, I found out he wasn't my real grandfather. But that seems irrelevant when he and I bathed in shafts of sunlight on slippery pine slopes laughing ourselves transparent.

In 1993, I went to Ohio University to study for my master's in linguistics and I was introduced to a student from Turkey. In that moment, all I'd read about Bulgarian history, all I was taught about the plight of the Bulgarian people under the yoke of the Ottoman Empire snowballed into a visceral sensation that paralyzed me. I couldn't get myself to shake his hand. I forced a nice-to-meet-you smile. I was stunned. What was embedded so deeply in my body that inhibited me from extending a hand? Just because he was Turkish? I didn't even grow up in Bulgaria.

He was a young man, like many of the friends I met there. How much more powerful this feeling must be for those who had steeped longer in our history? That reaction troubles me still. What took control over me? I've not stopped thinking about it even though we became friends and the moment faded.

I kept running into fragments of my family history. My biological grandfather died when my dad was one. He was stationed as an officer to fight in a swampy area near the Macedonian border. Only officers were given medicine to prevent malaria in the mosquito-infested trenches. He gave the pills to his soldiers, kept none for himself and contracted malaria.

Life went on after World War I. He was an engineer and part of the team that installed the first radio in Bulgaria. He assisted with shaping the radio media laws. He lectured and was the editor of a radio journal dedicated to the new technology. One day, instead of studying for my Latin exam, I looked up his publication in the national library in Sofia. *For the Radio Connoisseur* showed up hardbound in the small wood-panelled periodicals reading room. The year on the spine: 1926. It was a thrill to hold something my grandfather had created. I flipped through the yellowed pages and got lost in reading his editorials. I was an aspiring writer at the time and was communing with my grandfather. My parents were not too sure of this poetry stuff I was sharing with them. It was no way to make a living, they said. Today, my grandfather's name is in the radio history of Bulgaria. If the war hadn't happened, I would have been able to meet him. He died in 1940, at age forty-two, from complications of having had malaria. My dad does not remember his father and any attempt he made to find out about him was dramatically squashed by his mother (my grandmother). In his fifties, my dad met his half-sister (my aunt) who was fifteen at the time their father died. She was the child of his first wife, who had succumbed to cancer. Why did the families drift apart? The reasons are just for us to guess. A fifteen-year-old daughter and a new stepmother-wife who was under twenty living in the same home might not have been ideal. Did they get along? My father later got a stepfather (my step-grandfather), whom he had to accept as his dad. He could not get himself to call his stepfather dad. He called him uncle instead. In the will, he found out he was never adopted by the man he refused to call dad.

When we met, my dad's sister and I immediately fell in love with each other. She loved to write and travel and lived past her nineties with a spirit as wide as the world. The last time I saw her, she was in her late eighties and stayed overnight in Vancouver on her way to get on a cruise to Alaska.

I never got the chance to meet my maternal grandfather either. My mother was pregnant with me when he died. After serving in World War I, my mother's father studied to be a master printer. He almost came to Canada after the war. But no one wanted him to go and he didn't want to leave his family behind.

In 1923, while commuting between towns to get home, he was arrested. The September Uprising (considered to be Bulgaria's first anti-fascist revolt) was underway and military and police forces were on high alert, mobilized to subdue the uprising. He and other men were rounded up and locked in a basement. One of the guards began to shoot the prisoners one by one from a small window. When the man next to my grandfather was shot, he collapsed over him and bloodied both him and the man sitting on the other side of my grandfather. Something briefly distracted the gunman and when he resumed shooting, by sheer luck, he skipped the two men. Eventually, they were rescued by a group of rebels. For years, my grandfather and the man next to him got together on that date to celebrate the anniversary of that lucky twist of fate.

Bit by bit, the stories piled up from different sides and different members of my family. I was hungry for everything. I wanted to know where I come from. I felt less alien knowing both my grandfathers did what I have embraced with a passion: teaching, writing, editing and publishing.

After earning his master printer certificate in 1924, my maternal grandfather opened a printing shop and became the printer of his small town. His first wife died from tuberculosis. In 1940, he married my grandmother and the next year my mother was born. Her sister, the only aunt I knew as a child, was born a few years later in a basement while American planes bombed Sofia. Bulgaria happened to be on the side of Germany at the time—again on the wrong side. After World War II, the new government nationalized my grandfather's printing press and told him he could stay on as an employee. He survived all that but couldn't survive the mistake a nurse made at the hospital when she left the wrong food on his bedside table. He was admitted to the hospital with a perforated bleeding ulcer.

My mom remembers her dad walking to his print shop every day. Sometimes, she went hand in hand with him. At five, she knew how to read and write, to set the letters neatly, to nest them with little blackened fingers as if they were eggs about to hatch. At forty, I sent my mom a photo of the old printing press I found in the office of my first publisher and asked if that was the kind my grandfather had.

"The moment I saw the photo," she said, "I smelled the ink."

Then she told me how that spring she watched the birds build a nest in the linden tree below our balcony as if setting letters for a text we could learn to read.

My dad told us a few stories of his childhood. He refuses to write them down. In his head, they are always much better than written words. He remembers how the coal trains rattled through Sofia in the winter. It was a time of food and fuel shortages. He and his friends pulled their sleds along the train tracks and picked up the coal that fell from the train cars. They piled it on their sleds carefully lined with newspapers so nothing fell out, not even the black crumbs and dust. He was proud to bring home a little comfort to his family in the cold winter days. They said: *He brought the fire home.*

When the sirens went off, everyone headed for the bomb shelters. One time, it was just him and his grandfather in the house. My dad was about seven years old. He pulled on the old man's arm. His grandfather was hard of hearing. *Grandpa, let's get to the shelter.*

Grandpa would not budge. He thought my dad wanted to play with him so he shook him off. My dad ran and hid in the narrow water-meter shaft outside by the trash bins. He climbed down the metal brackets on the inside and pulled the lid closed. After the bombs died down, he pushed on the lid but couldn't lift it. He called and called until he lost his thin voice. Exhausted, he crouched at the bottom, straddled the trickle of water and drifted off to sleep. It was a small space. If a pipe had burst, it could have flooded the shaft and he would have drowned. If it weren't for the trickle of water at the bottom, he likely would have run out of air.

That day, a bomb fell on the cigarette factory across the street and left a crater in its wake. Rubble and shrapnel rained on top of the shaft, which made the lid too heavy for a child to lift. On the following day, while sorting through the debris and destruction, the neighbours heard him calling and dug him out. My great-grandfather never left the house. He thought what he heard was not bombs but potatoes popping on the stove. Later, the family dug their own shelter in the yard between the pear and the apricot trees. The kids played soldiers in the crater left where the cigarette plant used to be.

That same great-grandfather, who eventually went deaf, used to be a music teacher. My dad remembers him telling a story from the Balkan Wars, over and over, usually after dinner. The story told of how he was ordered to hold a mountain ridge with his rebel fighters. He saw his men die one after the other, including his best friend. They were outnumbered and desperate. He ordered the living to line up the dead every few metres, propped on rocks and trees with their helmets on, their guns pointing and ready. That way it would look like there was a row of soldiers ready to fight while the living retreated. A death chain, they called it. When the fighting resumed behind them, they saw fireworks of flesh and bone. The dead dying all over again. At the dinner table, wide-eyed, my dad listened. The story always ended with: *My best friend saved my life.*

At nine, my dad built his own crystal radio. He got the diagrams from the radio journal his dad edited. He gathered parts—coils, capacitor, detector, wires, whisker, headphones—and assembled them in an old candy box in his tiny room under the floor-to-ceiling painting of a plum tree ever blossoming. The plum tree painting covered a crack in the wall from ceiling to floor. At bedtime, he would turn the detector and tune in—Bill Haley, Paul Anka, Harry Belafonte—his contact with the world crystal clear. Through genetic translators, through wires, he connected even to his father, whom he dreamed of, whom he does not remember but wished he did.

War haunted the years I was growing up: through these stories, through my textbooks, through our military education in high school. A memory is suddenly there and I have to make sense of it. Even though I only spent a year in a Bulgarian school, I remember studying bombs, the different degrees of burns, what happens if an atom bomb is dropped. I especially remember the part where you should lie face down on the ground with your head pointing away from the blast and cover yourself with a white sheet. Memories lodged in my head like bullets. We had to pass exams on this material. I remember being graded on how fast we could assemble a Kalashnikov in grade eight, before we'd even learned to get along with one another. I would rather remember the boy who kissed me in the hallway after class one day. We shot at targets on cardboard boxes at the far end of our classroom, under glass-covered slogans above the blackboard—likely some bombastic statement about the future for which we were preparing. Our military education teacher was always in uniform and usually reeked of alcohol—as if he had to be drunk to do his job. We made fun of him. We were merciless with our jokes. One student said, "Why bother lying down? Just put the sheet over your head and run to the cemetery."

Don't look back. Look forward. My grandmother's voice echoes in my head. Each story an altar on which I burn a candle. I've lit many candles. Was this my grandmother's way of trying to spare me? I wanted to connect with her. I wanted to know where, how and with whom I belonged. What do I do with these memories? They are unlike any other part of my life. I wanted to know I am not a fragment but a link. I want to know how this past has made me who I am. The last time I saw her, she promised me photos and stories. I never got them. I go back to those birch woods to talk to my grandfather. I don't know where to go to talk to her.

Is This an Illness or an Accident?

The nurse at the university clinic seemed braced for some drama to unfold when she confirmed the pregnancy. I was pregnant with our first child. I wasn't sure how I felt either. It was 1996 and my husband and I were still completing our degrees. It was not like we were ready for a baby but we had decided not to try so hard *not* to have a baby. A couple of nights before, we were at a friend's birthday and my wine tasted like soap. I assumed it was the wineglass. As the baby-on-the-way news sank in, my husband beamed at me, which made both me and the nurse feel better.

❦

At the prenatal clinic, we were asked to fill out a student insurance form. The first question on the bright pink form was: *Is this an illness or an accident?*

We sat in the pink love seat in the waiting room and contemplated the given options. It was certainly not an illness. Not quite an accident. Still, accident was better than illness. We reluctantly checked accident and hoped that was the worst of it.

Next question: *Describe exactly what happened during the accident.*

We shared a good laugh, then strapped on our serious faces to figure out what to write in the pointed blanks. Every question that followed dug us deeper into the choice we'd initially made. Forms do that. Even when they claim multiple choice, they limit your options to, at best, a handful. Each choice we made limited what we could say further.

I don't remember how much the student insurance covered from the prenatal expenses and I don't remember if any birth expenses were covered, which was a good few more thousand dollars. That period was a paperwork blur. But $8,000 sounds about right. What I do remember is that my son was approaching two when we were still paying off his birth in monthly instalments. I was prepared for the burden of student loans but it looked like in the United States you were already in debt just by being born. Is that the original debt you add to your original sin?

All I knew of the United States before I ended up there in 1993 was that it was the place people went to dream the American dream. Athens, Ohio, didn't seem much of a dream. I was pursuing a master's degree at Ohio University instead. I needed a car to get to the dentist. Kroger—the huge grocery store—overwhelmed me. So much product, so much choice, so little of what I was used to calling food. It didn't smell or taste real and it was expensive. I arrived with $150 in my pocket, the money I got after I exchanged a whole summer's worth of earnings from a well-paid interpreting job at the ministry of education in Sofia. When I landed at the Columbus airport, I spent the night at the airport and had to wait for the shuttle from the university to pick me up the next day. In the morning, I craved a hot chocolate. When I saw the price of $1.50, I gave up. For someone who only had $150, that seemed expensive.

True, little Athens was a college town and unusually progressive for the area. The population roughly doubled with the incoming students, which made it bearable. The university was both a source of needed income and relief but also exacerbated economic disparity in a county often listed as the poorest in Ohio.

In syntax class, I met the man who became my husband. We met in the hallway before class. He was minoring in linguistics. I was considering submitting a poem to a contest for the first time and wanted someone other than my roommate to give me some feedback. I thought I'd ask him. I did not know him and he wasn't my type. Perhaps criticism from a stranger would hurt less than from a friend. He sat unsuspecting: a computer on his lap, long red hair cascading down his shoulders, jeans torn at the knees. Without hesitation, he pulled a pencil out and had some suggestions right away. I thought that was bold. I had forgotten that we met because of a poem.

Over time, I realized he was enamoured with me. I wasn't sure how I felt about him. As I navigated daily life, he was willing to assist with anything. A few months in, I realized he was always there when I needed him. He would borrow a car to drive me to that dentist. Life was better with him, fuller and sweeter. A definite improvement from the first American guy I dated who would only walk me halfway home. I walked the darker half on my own. He was a definite improvement from most guys I had dated up to that point. Once thought, these thoughts were hard to un-think. One day, over lunch break, we got a marriage licence. A week later, we were married by a judge. Two years later, we were in the clinic filling out insurance forms for our first child.

The merry-go-round with the Immigration and Naturalization Services (INS) was our next trial by paper. As a married couple, we applied for a green card. According to the INS, my husband was an American and I was an alien. Each time we had to deal with them required another piece of paper. Each piece of paper seemed to cost about $100. If you're lucky, you might be spared humiliation. It was an obstacle course of forms, a marathon without a trophy. Whoever created the forms surely didn't have me in mind. Was this why everyone in the waiting room sat in pairs? A pair appeared to consist of an alien (or a pod of aliens) and a lawyer. They went around attached by their accounts. The air filled with despair. How can you mean business if you aren't thousands of dollars in someone's debt? We were the wrong pair.

While in the green card process, we went abroad to visit my parents under the scrutinizing eye of the INS. We'd been married for a couple of years and I was five months pregnant. My husband was going to meet my parents for the first time. Initially, we planned to visit Bulgaria for our honeymoon but we used up our savings on the wedding. At that point, my parents didn't have enough time to get a visa to attend the ceremony.

A visa could take up to six months and it involved a substantial amount of paperwork on their end. It required letters on both sides stating (and in convincing ways) that my parents would go back to their country after they visited. It's best if you have property. Owning property seemed a better guarantee than your word. You might go back on your word, but you'll most likely go back to your property. You're attached to it through the umbilical cord of paperwork.

We were informed we couldn't leave the country without the permission of the INS while we were under the green card quarantine. We drove three hours to Cincinnati, Ohio, to visit the now painfully familiar sterile office. What we needed, they said, was an advance parole. It would cost about $95. Perhaps it was the word *advance* that threw me off, put my anxieties to sleep. As if adding the word *advance* in front of something like *parole* made it better somehow. That piece of paper was going to magically get us out and back in the country without a hitch. All seemed well. Our green card interview was scheduled within a week of our return. What they didn't tell us: the advance parole expired on the day of the interview, a few days after our return to the country. Nor did they tell us the implications of that.

We had a delightful trip to Bulgaria. My parents met their son-in-law for the first time and thankfully they liked him, long hair, earring and all. At that point, they did not have a lot of choice in the matter. We drove to the Black Sea. We visited the Rila Monastery and other favourite places. We made sure we had a layover in Prague, where we raced with the sunset so I could share more of what I loved before our love. We sat in the Staroměstské náměstí (Old Town Square), where we ate crepes the colour of skin under the medieval astronomical clock and licked our fingers with curiosity. The clock dates back to 1410. The trip here was not just across distance but across time; it makes a heart glad to know it belongs to ancient things we want to protect, things that inspire reverence. I miss that the most on the North American continent. Not much is sacred here and the value of most things are only indicated in a price tag. After our trip, we had to get back to the business of green card paperwork in the United States.

The interview was scheduled for eight in the morning. We drove down the night before and stayed at a motel. That way we didn't have to drive at ungodly hours or risk being late. We were ushered into an office, sat down before the muzzles of a camera and microphone. The man sitting across from us was framed by a photo in which he was posing with a German shepherd and a gun at the Mexican border. He proceeded with the interview. It was repetitive and debilitating. When I wasn't terrified of saying something wrong or inconsistent, I tried to imagine what this man did when he left work. Who did he go home to? Who were his friends? What were his passions? What gets him up in the morning? Behind him was also a portrait of former President Bush Senior. One wall was covered by a painfully square map of the city of Cincinnati, full of straight lines. Just like the questions. You answer them in straight lines. The only detours here would be the ones they ask you to take. Only stop at the traffic lights the interviewer controlled. Fasten your seat belts for sudden and sharp U-turns. Don't duck down suspicious alleyways. That was when I started noticing the fear fairies dancing everywhere—on the edges of his words, on anything we said. The letters on the pages before us, and the spaces between, were crawling with them. I'll get to know them well over time, my fear-ies.

When we were done, the officer sent us out into the waiting room. He held onto my passport, which I found unnerving. We weren't allowed to leave. My husband and I were not supposed to talk to each other. I hadn't eaten yet. I was six months pregnant. It was noon. After what seemed like forever, the officer came out to declare that I don't have a visa and from that point on I'm illegal in the country. I assumed he meant after 12 noon. Otherwise, why didn't he tell us such momentous news at the interview that morning at 8 a.m.? Had I left and returned on my student visa, I wouldn't be in trouble now. The advance parole had expired. He made it clear that unless we filled out another form, paid another $100, they would start deportation procedures. I was pregnant, hungry, thirsty and getting upset. I had a gun-loving man holding my passport open with his fist in my face while at the same time withholding it. He was dictating my future. I wasn't taking sufficient notes. If paperwork is painful at the best of times, try filling it out on an empty stomach, growling for two, dizzy with weakness. And we did just that.

This only appeased things for about an hour when a woman officer, whom we hadn't even met yet, addressed us in the staccatos of impatience. She announced to me, but mostly to the whole waiting room, that it's clear from the answers I'd given (in the form I had just filled out under duress) that I had no idea what I was doing. She sprinkled in the word *deportation* a few times for good measure. We found ourselves in another back office after we walked through a narrow dark hallway. When I attempted to ask questions to figure out what it is they wanted of me, she told me to be quiet until she was done with her spiel. By the time she was done, I had forgotten my questions. The fearies were working overtime and for less than minimum wage. Their wings made such a loud *whoosh* in my ears that I couldn't hear much beyond their pounding. At least, at that point, we had a visa and we could go home.

This long-distance relationship with the INS was wearing us down. Every visit meant taking time off work, a three-hour drive each way and likely booking a hotel. You do what they say or else they take out their long INS sticks and beat you to the border.

In Margaret Ball's *Mathemagics,* Riva is an alien from an alternate reality who brings her daughter to Earth, the Planet of the Paper-Pushers, to educate her.[2] I'm not much for Chicks in Chainmail novels; not my choice for a book but it was a gift from my husband's aunt and he read it to me at bedtime. *I* was that alien. I had come to study in the United States from an alternate reality and spent most of my time figuring out how to dodge the attacks of the paper-pushers. There's always that moment where you want to know exactly what they want you to say so you can appear normal, blend in, keep yourself up on the social high wire. If you stand out too much, a paper-pusher puts the magnifying glass on you and holds it there until it burns. If you come to them with one problem, you'll likely walk away with two. If they ill-advised you, it's still your problem. Chances are, by the time they are done with you, you'll have done something wrong—or, God forbid, something illegal. It's always by their definition. If not now, then after you complete that next form. You'll surely slip and they'll catch you. Was this an accident or an illness? We kept checking boxes, circling options on forms, getting pushed further into the margins. The margins didn't demand anything from me but they were also getting narrower. I began to dwell there and spent a lot of time writing in them.

The next thing I knew, we needed to visit the INS again. Probably a good year had passed in between but to me it felt constant. This is reminiscent of the night I gave birth (the birth we were still paying off). Six hours or so into labour, the doctor kept inducing in me the fear that if I kept going the way I was, I'd have no energy to push the baby out. That was after they gave up trying to induce contractions right after my water broke. I resisted their onslaughts, waited for my perfectly good body to do what it knew how to do. I breathed with focus, exercised my agency as a body capable of giving birth. The nurse tempted me with a lovely cocktail of drugs in the IV.

"It'll give you the chance to rest," the nurse said.

The doctor tapped his watch and said, "You're the fourth baby tonight. We don't have all night."

But I *did* have all night. The first time they offered me drugs, I refused, danced around with my IV to ward them off. I asked for a Tylenol instead. The phlebotomist (whom we nicknamed Vampire) found that amusing. She humoured me and gave me a Tylenol. I promptly threw it up. They expected me to labour sitting in bed at a forty-five-degree angle watching TV. Everything in the room rolled away from me except the blanket rack on the wall. The one solid thing I held onto.

This is the way I felt with all the paperwork. Each time you feel you are holding onto something real or rooted it rolls away from you. Eventually, they surrounded me with enough fear and I gave in. The moment I thought I was in pain, I truly *was* in pain. And the more painful I thought it was, the more painful it got. I said okay to the drugs.

Their cocktail made me argumentative, even more ponderous and philosophical. For years later, we laughed when my husband reminded me of the questions I asked: "What's the point of the past?" and, "What is time?" I asked while my husband dug his thumbs and fists in my back as I lay on my side: the one thing that gave me relief.

I would ask, "Are you comfortable?"

He would say, "Yes, I am."

"No, you're not," I would counter. "You're lying to me."

He couldn't type for a week after that night. What the drugs also did was make me drift off between contractions. I only woke up for the peak of each one. I couldn't tell how far apart they were; to me, they felt like one constant peak. The only moments I was brought back into consciousness were the moments I was in pain. That is how the INS visits felt to me: peak after peak, with no memorable relief in between.

This time we had to apply to stay in the country under the clause of *exceptional hardship*. One of my education grants required me to go back to Bulgaria after graduating and work there for two years. At that time, we couldn't fulfil that requirement. My circumstances had changed: I was married, my husband had student loans to pay off, we had a baby to pay off and our baby was also being treated for a heart problem. What complicated things further was the fact that there was no mechanism to pay back the grant. So, that wasn't an option. Their response? I should go back to Bulgaria on my own, leave my newborn and husband in the United States. They are American after all.

I raised the common-sense voice of concern: "But a baby needs his mom."

This was drowned out by: "You'll have to prove that in court."

This, over months of correspondence and paperwork. Even the president of the university tried to intercede on our behalf, as did the senator's office. That made no difference; the INS wasn't answerable to congress.

In the meantime, on TV the American president and politicians gave speeches glorifying family values. I would think the first of those was to keep families together? When my brain began to hurt with this unsolvable conundrum, I phoned a lawyer. He talked to me for ten minutes and charged me $150. He translated the situation into language I still couldn't comprehend; this time not because the words were unclear, but because it now seemed like a cruel joke. I knew by then the INS didn't have a sense of humour.

"What they want is for you to prove in court that a child needs its mother for the first two years of life," he said, sounding like he also had a hard time believing it.

"They're kidding, right?" I said.

"No," he said. "They are serious." This verified my suspicion that not only is there no place for humour but also no place for humanity in this transaction.

"But how does one prove that in court? I thought... that's... common sense."

His response? "You hire a child psychologist."

I deflated. "The odds?"

"You have about a sixty percent chance of winning the case."

"How much would all this cost?" I asked.

"Very likely about $15,000," he said.

Common sense seemed to cost a lot in the United States. Still, the $150 we paid him was worth every cent. That was the moment I was convinced it wasn't worth winning at this rigged game.

If I'm that unwelcome here, why fight to stay in this country? I fell in love here but I didn't love it here. I thought I was strong enough to survive the onslaught of paperwork and the psychological fallout. I've had to deal with bureaucracy in other oppressive regimes where your fate hung on the goodwill of the person on the other side of the desk. This wasn't that different except goodwill was taken out of the equation. The money we paid for each piece of paper was reminiscent of bribery except here it was legal. After six years, I was still an alien and treated like a criminal. Why would I want to raise my children here? It was easier to get a gun than a hot lunch at school, no good affordable health care and, as I'd just reconfirmed, there was too little common sense. The more I played the game, the more it cost my family, both financially and emotionally. For too many years we'd been measuring our freedom in pieces of paper.

The verdict was in: *I was in the wrong country.* There was instant relief in these thoughts. I didn't want their "greed" card. I gave them a red penalty card instead. We changed the game and the rules. Fortunately, we could afford that move.

We didn't need to hire a lawyer to immigrate to Canada. We asked questions online and were surprised when lawyers replied to our queries and didn't send us a bill. We didn't need to prove in court that a family needs to stay together. We needed to show we had $10,000 to our name but we got to keep the money. My husband liked the West Coast and eventually wanted to move there anyway. Vancouver was about as far as we were willing to drag our stuff. In other words, it took us no time to decide to leave this godforsaken country.

The year and a half before we left for good was about as comfortable as holding a hot pan with oil about to burst into flames. We had to sever ties with our life in Athens, sell the house we bought the year before, terminate the part-ownership my husband had in a restaurant. We had to move to Columbus for my husband's new job. There was a lot to do. Most of it involved paperwork.

We had a wish list for the place we wanted to rent in Columbus while we were finalizing our separation from Athens. Of all the things we had on that list, sidewalks rose to the top of the list, became our priority. I didn't drive. Had we taken sidewalks for granted? I wanted to be able to get out of the house and go for a walk with my toddler. We found only one place where you could walk out of your door and step onto a sidewalk instead of a parking lot. True, people didn't pick up after their dogs, it was hard to play in the grass, but there were sidewalks. True, the highway was right behind us, loud as ever, but there were sidewalks. We didn't have to drive to go for a walk.

I was still on a student visa, which required me to be in school full-time. Distance and small child prevented me from attending to my doctorate degree full-time. Every communication with the Canadian immigration office was a little vessel of hope. Any day, the INS or related authorities could knock on my door. The fearies moved into our home, beat their leathery wings about the house. I paid them nothing but they were used to hovering on the poverty line. The sound of those days was the sound of a bomb ticking. You couldn't diffuse it. You didn't know how much time you had left. A Schrödinger's bomb. Such uncertainty was debilitating.

Each chapter of *Mathemagics* was a complex mathematical formula supposed to add up to the numerical value of the chapter. I never did the calculations. What if it didn't add up? Eventually, your paperwork will not add up. You'll muck it up somehow. You'll contradict yourself. Memory, imprecise and imperfect, becomes your enemy, never adds up to a neat and perfect number. The memory of paper is perfect. Your complex life cannot hold court and make counter arguments. Forms are blind. I often wrote in the margins in hope someone might veer into understanding my circumstance better. The margins were narrower than ever. There was now another voice eating away at the margins: *Anything you say can, and will, be used against you*. So, the less you say, the better. The fearies claimed the margins too. These fearies are not cute with fluffy wings as in *A Midsummer Night's*

Dream. They are reptilian and slippery, slithering through the unguarded spaces of your mind. They crawl under barbed wire, enter through keyholes, gates left ajar, crevices leading into your home. *A Midsummer Nightmare*. They'll survive ice, breathe under water, live through a fire. They'll wear down your resistance, tattoo your thoughts and heart, change who you are. Your tears cannot drown them. Even as I write this, I can hear the snap of leathery wings and whispers.

We got our landing papers in 1999, loaded our worldly possessions on a truck and drove 4,000 kilometres across the country to the Peace Arch border crossing. The moment we landed, I felt I was home even though I'd never been to Canada before. The highways shrank from six or eight lanes to two, the clouds were spectacular, a few storeys high, and the green was more intense than I'd seen for a while. Or ever. My vision had been reduced to black and white those six years I spent in the United States. Colours seen with a mind at peace seemed more radiant. As we drove toward Vancouver, I realized I had never felt at home in Athens or Columbus. Not even for one day out of the six years we lived there. (And it hurts to call that living.) It was like being born again after a very long labour. Twenty-five years later, this feeling hasn't changed. The sidewalks are endless, public transit is abundant, and health care doesn't bankrupt you. It cost us nothing to give birth to my second child. Here, people don't call me an alien. I rarely get asked where I come from. When people bother to ask, they think I'm from Montreal. This might be as close to home as it gets.

Detour: The Ghost of Paperwork Past

In 2004, while my parents were visiting from Bulgaria, we went to see my sister in Portland. At the border, we got pulled over and sent to the main office. I was sure it was something to do with my parents. I was a Canadian citizen now. We went in. Waited. The young border guard peered into the computer screen with a stern look, a furrow in his brow. He glanced at me a few times. He went to get an older officer. The two officers leaned their heads into the screen, exchanged the word *parole* a few of times, eyed me again. I was the one they were scrutinizing. My old friends the fearies made an appearance. A familiar paperwork ghost had come back to haunt me. The word *parole* was somehow still attached to my name. Looks like it was not *advance* anymore. The older officer waved his hand, dismissed it with, "This is a leftover from the old system." I hung onto his words as if they were a rope over the crater left in the aftermath of the paperwork eruption before 1999. Then, he went about his business. We were free to go. The fearies reside now at the border, hover around my head each time I cross. We have a reunion about once a year. I don't know what it'll take to get rid of them.

To Neighbour or Not to Neighbour

Under a City Government that Only Wakes Up from the Developer's Kiss

We landed in Canada in 1999. The person who was supposed to meet us with the keys at the condo we rented in Richmond was not picking up their phone. We waited a whole day for the keys to arrive. We walked around, homeless, pretending to sightsee. In the evening, our new neighbour lifted his child through the small kitchen window and got us into our condo. The truck with our possessions wasn't due for another week so he lent us a futon, a lamp and dishes to ease the wait. The keys arrived after we broke into our already rented apartment. Was the landlord not as local as we thought? As wonderful as that neighbour was, there was no sense of community there. One person does not a neighbourhood make. Our door opened onto a parking lot and the units embraced the asphalt as if it were precious.

A year later, with a second child on the way, we decided to look for a house with a yard. We couldn't afford one anywhere near jobs, even with our $120,000 family income. Each time we crossed a bridge, property prices dropped; we settled for a place in Maple Ridge, about an hour drive from Vancouver. The realtor called it a bedroom community, which I did not understand. They were building a theatre, which tipped some scales in our heads of potential arts and culture in the area.

Our house was on a street without sidewalks. I was either on the road negotiating cars or trespassing. We had to drive to daycare. Except I couldn't drive. We took the bus, which came every thirty minutes. Except it didn't always come. I had to learn to drive. But I didn't want to. My husband commuted to Vancouver three hours a day on the West Coast Express—the commuter train that tipped the scales for us to move there. The train ran to the downtown core in the morning and came back in the evening. Not having much family time was taking a toll.

Living in Maple Ridge reinforced the rule: high fences make good neighbours. That way, Bob couldn't judge my moss-and-dandelion yard, though I could still hear the obsessive leaf blowing and lawn mowing. That way, I couldn't see him pouring poisons in his lawn and he couldn't feel sorry for me when I picked dandelion leaves for my salad.

After three years, we sold the house and moved to False Creek South, across the water from where my husband worked. Ironically, the grand opening of Maple Ridge's theatre was on the very day we left. I wrote two poems about those three years, one of which was called "serving time in the burbs." My love affair with Maple Ridge was over. True, I could write in the cafes there, but there was something wrong about coffee houses that sat empty. I began to understand the meaning of a bedroom community and I did not like it one little bit. *Community* did not seem to be the right word.

We found a market rental in Vancouver a few blocks from where we live now. It advertised itself as "affordable" but it wasn't. Elvis, the maintenance guy, made it bearable. When I told him about a problem, he raised a finger, as if checking which way the wind was blowing, and said, "I have a solution." Then he brought bleach. Bleach was the solution to most problems.

He loved Mars bars and stories. That fuelled our connection and got me to the top of the solutions queue. My bedroom window opened onto the walkway around the outside of the building; I kept my blinds shut. The building across blocked the sun from shining in. My kids called my bedroom the cave. The day we moved out, we found a layer of fuzzy mould all over the back of my dresser.

I liked the courtyard, where children played, but frequent all-night parties echoed between our building and the seniors' home. The good-neighbour policy in that concrete-windows-sweating fishbowl was: residents don't intend to stay long enough to care about their neighbours. We applied to a number of co-ops in the area. Three years later, we moved into False Creek Housing Co-op.

Children have a freedom here that is rare: they play in the courtyard under the watchful eyes of the residents in the units, which all face inward. It's hard to feel lonely, or invisible, in pathways and spaces designed for interaction. We walked and biked to school and daycare. When we crossed Laurel Street land bridge from Charleston Park, we told stories, bounced off rocks and manoeuvred around off-leash dogs instead of worrying about the traffic on Sixth Avenue racing to the next light.

Co-op living was a huge relief after Maple Ridge and Columbus, Ohio, where finding a place with sidewalks was hard, let alone a playground, and where it was not uncommon to see kids on leashes, or folded and strapped in umbrella strollers, for convenience. Where off-the-highway, drive-in complexes looked more like truck rest stops and motels than neighbourhoods. Co-op living was too good to be true.

When I speak in favour of co-op housing, I'm often treated as if I am not working hard enough to afford a house. As if it's a developmental stage I have to go through to get to the finish line of owning a home. This myth is important to promote in a culture that venerates private property. I chose *not* to own a house after I realized that my house owned me; I'd become a slave to my property. Then, I became a slave to high rent in market rentals where community was near impossible to build, in a city that gambles with our lives and neighbourhoods.

Over the years, we watched buildings come down and go up across Sixth Avenue. My younger son was enamoured with a heritage house he named the Owl House (named after the owls on the roof). He watched as it got stripped down, propped on stilts and wrapped in blue tarps. We worried it wouldn't survive while concrete went up all around it. The Owl House was built in 1894 and currently houses Caffè Cittadella. It was lucky to survive. What'll happen to character and almost-heritage buildings, family memory, neighbourhood memory, lifetimes, if rezoning fails to protect them? Do you have something in your neighbourhood you wish to protect? Don't wait.

Our identity began to transform in our co-op community. We mapped our neighbourhood on foot. Memories were embedded in landmarks. When you commit to a place, it's easier to build continuity and sense of belonging. It's easier to protect what you care about. But it doesn't work if the city keeps destroying what we build with care. We need to build with the intent that things will last, the way this neighbourhood was built in the 1970s. False Creek South is on the top-ten watch list for 2020 at Heritage Vancouver.

Of course, it is not always perfect. We do have a good-neighbour policy but that is only as good as the neighbour. I found that the place did not have a smoking policy and I had to count on the good-neighbour policy for that. In my twenty years living here, the failure to communicate with a smoking neighbour is the only failure I feel. It is hard to tell a smoker to stop smoking under my nose or under my window when the smoke filters through the pipes into other units. I am not the only one who has to deal with it but I am the one who failed to come to a resolution, in the absence of good will from my neighbour. We have much bigger issues to attend to with the lease renewals so this one is still on the back burner. Perhaps good-neighbour policies are only meant for good neighbours, the way locks keep mostly honest people out.

During the pandemic, the benefits of living in a co-op became even more apparent. Beyond merely being affordable, the co-op supports mutual aid as well as physical and mental well-being. It's what gets us through hard times. Our city should be interested in preserving this kind of resilient living to spare itself the expenses that result from the unhealthy housing environments it creates. We need housing built independent of the market's volatility. Every group benefits but vulnerable populations, low-income families, children and seniors, who are lucky to age in place, benefit most of all. Had I taken it for granted that a person can live in one place for forty years and not have to move if they do not want to?

In 1972, the visionary False Creek South plan was derided as too dense for a viable community. Today, the city is undertaking a redevelopment of False Creek South, which is on "city land."[3] We don't know what the fate of our co-op housing complex will be in this well-established mixed community. In the 1970s, city planners aimed for a socially mixed housing of varied incomes. That was unheard of at the time. Fifty years later, that vision remains a success. Our long-term leases have protected us from the municipal and market tampering and greed. Now that the leases are expiring, the city is trying to redefine what a co-op is and tie our housing charges to external metrics instead of putting policy in place to sustain and support the affordability that co-ops have managed in a market now gone haywire. In 1974, the *Vancouver Sun* reported a member of the city's False Creek planning team quit, calling the proposed development "a blunder of classic proportions" deemed to end up as a slum.[4] Time proved this city planner wrong.

How affordable is your rent? The quality of our life depends on it. Urban design shapes how we live and who we become. It dictates who you will (or won't) connect with, it tells you where to walk and it affects the memory of an entire city. Co-ops embrace culturally, ethnically and financially diverse populations; the co-ops on the Creek cater predominantly to families. It allows us to live and work near our communities, not be forced into the peripheries or to leave the city, disconnected from what we've learned to call home. Over the last hundred years, Vancouver has not matured into a city that is ethically and morally responsible for its medium-to-lower-income residents. It's perverse to think forced mobility is a choice. The Little Mountain tragedy is our nightmare. The Olympic Village fiasco is our fear. Unless land speculation stops and the jacking up of land value is curbed, the city will continue to erase communities and bleed people out of Vancouver.

The people who built and sustained this co-op are aging in place. They've seen a few generations grow and thrive here. We owe them the respect and the care they need to age in their community. But when the co-op was built, did people think they would grow old here? Perhaps they did not believe the co-op would last for fifty years. Now, we need to build units for our seniors, for our young adults, to be able to free more units for new families. It is the minimum we can do as we continue to defend our right to sustain and provide deeply affordable homes.

My sons' confidence grew in the many ways they could be independent in and around the co-op. They engaged with a diverse group of multi-aged youth, adults, seniors and elders. They learned to negotiate unstructured play time, made rules, coordinated games and learned to manage their bodies, emotions and minds. They contributed to a community. "The best way to equip kids to handle challenges in their lives is to help them learn how to develop and maintain strong social networks within supportive communities," says Elin Kelsey in her book *Hope Matters*, and this is even more important in a climate-change future.[5] Countless experts now say existing housing is more affordable (and environmentally conscious) than any newly built affordable housing. This is even more true now that everything has become a lot more expensive. Well-established neighbourhoods are best left undisturbed even if densification work is done with infill and in alignment with neighbourhood values.

Since we moved to Canada, this is the longest we've been able to live in one place. For the past twenty years, we have integrated our lives into a close-knit social fabric and we are better for sticking with it. In 2017, twelve-year-old Sirus Grames-Webb told council, "If you look at False Creek, that's what a city should look like, it's the perfect image for planners... Ask any kid who lives here, they'll tell you how awesome our False Creek neighbourhood is. You should make more places in Vancouver like this."[6] So, why has the city not replicated this elsewhere? There's so much demand. My sons spoke to council in 2021 along with over a hundred other people against pushing a real estate plan that treated the area as if it was a blank piece of land.

When we talk about housing in our co-op, we mean a community that embraces itself, the way the two enclaves of our co-op embrace the courtyard space where we gather and play. A place we're happy to volunteer to improve and sustain. In fact, it is crucial we all contribute to the upkeep. A better wealth comes with investing in social capital. That is the essence of a co-op. My children learned more from being part of a co-op community than they learned in school. The report city staff sent to council does not reflect any of that; the city has no metric to account for this social capital and community wealth. They love numbers, quantity more than quality. Often, quality is abandoned altogether. We discovered they also did not really have good information or data on the people who live in these co-ops. They made their decisions from the lens of finance and real estate. Often, not only do we not have possibilities for community building in Vancouver but we also have poor buildings to not do it in. We don't have another forty years to wait for city hall to catch up. Our lease will expire in twelve years.

We say time will tell. This is one instance in which time has told. The proof is in the success. Co-ops are a solution, a successful and healthy expression of non-profit housing. If we built only co-ops from now on, we still wouldn't have enough for decades to come.

The children under my window are negotiating the rules of the next game. They'll negotiate until they get it right. There's no game otherwise. We now have to figure out the rules of the game the management at city hall is playing and make sure they play fair. In the meantime, we are left wondering what'll happen to this most successful model of a neighbourly hood.

This is the longest place I have lived in so far. A co-op gives us security of tenure. And that makes me feel like I am closer to having arrived *home*.

Stairway to Haven

As summer break approaches, I am often asked: *Are you going away this summer?* Each time, the question startles me. My first thought usually is: *Why go somewhere else when I have been looking forward to being right here? When here is where I have been travelling to all my life?*

The light here already dances so perfectly on mountain slopes, on the surfaces of city and water. Here, the land and the ocean embrace me, the trees and the crows call to me. Why travel 7,000 kilometres away to find a place like this rooftop patio? Every summer, I am enchanted all over again with the place I now call home. All this, of course, is awkward to utter in passing on the bus or in a split second shared with a co-worker.

I wait for summer the way a famished person is intent on lunch. Those long evenings on the patio when the sun takes forever to set and nothing rushes it along. It sits and visits, lingers—stays for dinner. It is a focussed, aware kind of waiting. Here, on False Creek South, patio time in the summer is sacred, non-negotiable. The way traffic lights are non-negotiable, the way weather is non-negotiable.

When does patio season begin? There comes a day in late May or early June when I rush upstairs and know: *This is it!* And just as the journey toward summer is purposeful and long, so begins the journey from my front door to the rooftop patio—the longest journey I take each day. My life plays out in between.

I unlock my front door and enter the dining room; here, we greet and share meals. Farther into our home is the galley kitchen where food steams and brews, sizzles and boils. I spend so much time in the kitchen I jokingly refer to it as my second office. (Okay, maybe it is not a joke.) Seven steps up is the living room where another big slice of life unfolds. We lounge and talk. My sons play cello, guitar, mandolin, piano. We watch movies, share stories and candlelight. We also argue and regularly forget to water the plants on the balcony.

Another seven steps and I am at my bedroom door. The one place I have neglected lately in favour of the rest of the house. My king-sized bed is the island I take refuge on amidst the sea of unorganized things. The walls here are thinner, especially on mornings when I try to sleep in. Another flight of seven steps and I come to the kids' rooms. Under the skylight, the gable, the slanted roof that rises to a point, they grow. Whatever they outgrow ends up on this landing. Plenty to distract me here too. Finally, the last eight steps lead me up to the hatch in the roof that opens onto the patio. Once I have stepped over this threshold, I have arrived at the patio I share with my neighbours.

Amidst the lichen and mosses, the brilliant yellow blooms of the gold sedum among the pebbles and rocks, next to the uninvited fern, I sit in a folding chair, barefoot on the weather-worn boards. Only my books, journal, wine and a bowl of apricots, blueberries or cherries will accompany me here. The taste of summer, at last, under a long stretch of sunset, followed by the river of crows at dusk, as punctual as a clock. Sometimes, they fly in the shape of a poem I am writing, the way my words stream down the page.

In August, the sun is aligned perfectly for the maximum splash of light, unlike in autumn and winter when it slips too soon behind the tree to the right or the roof to the left. I hold onto these summer days in winter when it gets dark mid-afternoon, when November rains plague us for weeks, when, in December, we have been under cloud cover for what feels like months. Daylight is pale and thin as it inches along furniture, shifts between paintings and bookshelves. A rare splash of sun on a wall blooms briefly into a winter canvas. I savour these bright visits. I keep very busy during the dark seasons, comforted by the thought that the endless days of summer are travelling towards me.

Sometimes, my kids come up to the patio and we have dinner here. Sometimes, my neighbour is also busy doing what I am doing: getting away from it all. Sometimes, we talk. Sometimes, we negotiate the wasps, the short-lived winged ants. But mostly, business stays below. The quiet here comes with gifts: the bee buzzing around a lavender flower fills my attention to the brim, the swish of crows' wings as they fly low overhead claims all of me. Sometimes, music drifts across the water from a jazz festival, planes hum in the sky, children's voices rise from the courtyard, negotiating tag, capture the flag or some game invented on the spot. Children's voices have replaced the songs of birds on False Creek. We hear so few. The chickadees' lonely calls at dawn and dusk pull notes of nostalgia so deep memory scrambles frantically to remember what it is missing. And in that process, moments unfurl like new leaves, become polished like river pebbles.

By July, the race to the patio has established itself. The hunger for this refuge of renewal is as ripe as the cherry tomatoes the crows track with a sharp eye. I come up here with anticipation, never hesitation. This place remains unburdened by agendas. I can exist here without, and beyond, comparison. If I want to watch a bee or an ant, I can and do. I read and write and daydream. One summer, I ordered all the Leonard Cohen books I could find. After three hundred pages and a glass of wine, I was not sure which one of us had written the poems in my journal that night.

we are not floorboards that are nailed
we are not tiles that are fixed
we are not self-proclaimed
self-sacrificing protagonists…

See what I mean.

Here, I can ask myself difficult questions and be honest with the answers. They stay between me, the moss, the bees and the crows. Here, I am gently pushed and pulled by fragments of truth salvaged from the day's debris the way the feather reed grasses are swayed by the warm summer breeze. These grasses are loved and tended. My neighbour, Jan, has been growing them for years.

In the hours that follow, the sun is an attentive lover, caresses me from head to toe, kisses the way only August light can kiss. In an attempt to meet my gaze, the burning orb descends to eye level, grows tender, displays the patience of stars. A gaze still so intense I can only steal a glimpse or two out of the corner of my eye as it lingers on my eyelashes, makes me blush. I sit illuminated in this warm late evening glow, its gold and silk.

This place is my sun church with its altar of light. I can hear myself think between sips of full-bodied wine and bursts of raspberries on the tongue. Here, I can sit with disappointment, pain and grief until the answers to yesterday's questions boil over the copper edge of the horizon. I feed on morsels of fruit and something small realized. It is easier here to transform despair into something filigreed and delicate I can take downstairs into the life this city shapes for me. We play a strange game of hide-and-seek here, God and I, in which we both want to be found. We leave our fingerprints everywhere. I am surprised again and again by the great sense of peace that settles into me after these hours on my patio.

Yes, my life continues to play out between the front door and the twenty-nine steps to my little rooftop sanctuary. The possibility for numerous distractions is there with each step up and I am compelled to check off one more box on my to-do list, to put one more thing back in its place. Yet, things fall into place so easily in the hours spent in stillness in the one place that does not ask anything of me.

In the summer, I pursue the patio the way one pursues a life goal. The boundaries between worlds blur. More becomes possible next to the self-planted, fragile saxifrage that creeps innocently over the rocks while deep in its name sleeps the idea of stone breaker. Thoughts expand in the setting sun, grow as nuanced as the sunset. The heart that can lose its way, can open here to hold more and everything all at once. How quickly it regains its unfathomable capacity for understanding and compassion even though it is only as big as a tight fist. I feel myself grow more generous, kinder, wiser in the delicate evening exhale of the rosemary, lavender, grasses and fig tree. I dream of a grapevine arbour to sit under and in my mind, it has already climbed up the trellis. This summer, I might finally plant it.

The seasons circle back to the question: *Where are you going this summer?* The question assumes I am going away. It suggests that the one who asks is perhaps looking forward to getting away. I know it is just small talk, so small it is not worth a second thought. I also know that language shapes us and when we keep repeating something over and over, we end up believing it. That question is about as annoying as people who complain about the weather all year round. For one who travels for work, staying home is a lot more alluring. For one who has moved all her life, staying in one place is an accomplishment.

It is true the bustle of the big city is only four blocks away. The city's anger and pain quietly simmer under the pressure lid of survival. This is a city that often stuns me with its impatience, with its desire to destroy and replace beautiful buildings with ones that have no imagination or identity. A city that thinks it can live off its real estate forever. A city that forgets it does not own but exploits stolen land and that this prosperity does not belong to it. A city that forgets that we need public spaces designed to inspire our generosity. All this and more follows me up to the patio like a puppy starved for attention. I let it circle and circle until it finds a place to lie down.

The self is so happy to sway and buzz here in the summer breeze, to take leaps at the horizon, to enjoy the quiet space, to compose itself, to stitch its scattered and frayed pieces back together amidst the fragrant petunias and barbecue wafting from the balconies below.

As a child, I remember the smell of the ocean, how it was always the first sign that we had arrived, that we were on vacation. My patio is about one hundred steps from the edge of the water. When the tide goes out, the smell is strong and pungent. I inhale deeply. It never fails to take me back to my childhood. Add to that the call of seagulls and ripe peaches dripping down the chin and the sense that I am on vacation blossoms anew, even if it is for but a few hours.

Yes, the journey to my rooftop patio has many steps, but once here, time stops. And I can be present for each eternal moment.

And I can keep coming back no matter what the day serves or severs. The little fig tree my neighbours gave me is now over four feet, four soles high. It keeps coming back even after a deep freeze and a drought. Its dark shiny leaves open like palms. Here next to it, I, too, become an open palm.

Children of the Trees

This past summer, I watched two dozen cedars slowly die outside my window. In a matter of months, they turned from green to rust, stood like candles ready to be lit on a day of mourning. I watched men with chainsaws climb them, slice them and feed them to the wood chipper. I sat behind my glass door in vigil. These trees have defined our horizon for as long as we've lived here. Each time I sit to write, we nod to each other across Sawyers Lane, Cedars and I.

Before the stump grinder arrived a week later, there was a bouquet of flowers on one stump, a pair of shoes on another. I wasn't alone in my mourning. During the summer of 2019, over a hundred cedars came down along False Creek, one of the few urban forests around. For months, the chainsaws screamed, the chippers shredded. Each time, they triggered a chain reaction of worry and grief that has taken grip of me in all the devastation. More cedars are coming down today. Too dry for cedar, the sawyer said when I asked. Too dry for cedar in cedar country.

All my life, I have dragged bits of nature into my house—pebbles, shells, twigs, logs, twisted driftwood, rusty river rocks. As if they were life giving. And they were. As if I needed them closer than outside. They remind me where life comes from.

Coloured leaves and four-leaf clovers I pressed decades ago still fall out of the pages of books. As if they were not the outside but more like the inside of what I call home. As if that is what books are made of. And they are. We are entangled with trees whether we acknowledge it or not, even if the only tree embrace some feel today is in the wood frames of their beds.

"We are made and remade from the breath of trees" scientist and researcher Diana Beresford-Kroeger reminds us in her book *Our Green Heart*.[7] We need these reminders as the distance between inside and outside grows. In the lockdown of a pandemic, I was advised that even five minutes under a tree will change my mood and my outlook. And, of course, it does. But I already know that. I *feel* the need for it. Ideally, you are reading this essay under a tree. If not, please put the book down and spend at least five minutes under a tree.

One enters the world by admiring it. French philosopher Gaston Bachelard says, "The poet no longer describes; he exalts."[8] It is this feeling I get when I'm among the trees. I am interested in how wonder and awe are a point of entry, how admiration makes that which is admired the best it can be. Be that a child or a tree. Bachelard also says, "It is non-sense to claim to study the imagination objectively since one receives the image only if one admires it."[9] What if we were to study the imagination subjectively? But isn't that what poets do? Bachelard also says that imagination is a tree, which perhaps means we cannot study trees objectively either. And if we do, we rob them of their being-ness, deny that they are a powerful web of life support we depend on—a fact we've become too arrogant to remember.

Perhaps, we'll remember when we no longer have the luxury to stand under a tree and look at the world from there.

In one of my poems, I say, "We are the children of the trees."[10] That line surprised me close to two decades ago but the more I think about it, the more I recognize that what I know intuitively science is now reaffirming. We would not be here if it were not for the trees. Trees watch over us. They hold us in their gaze. And if they look away, we fall.

I climbed trees as a child. Spent endless untraceable hours in them. Growing up in Nigeria, I climbed most of the neem trees on the periphery of our yard. I picked tomatoes, peppers or guavas from the garden, got a book and hid in my favourite tree with branches conveniently shaped like a seat. That tree arched its back over the road by the fence and I watched the world below go by. Our swing hung from a tree. My closest encounter with a snake was hanging upside down in a tree. Eye to eye, the snake (likely deadly poisonous) and I hung there in the balance. That might also have been the fastest descent from a tree I have performed.

My friendships with trees were as special as my childhood friendships. To this day, I dream with them, think with them. Their dendritic neurons shape thoughts that obsess me. So few of the school-aged children I teach have climbed a tree or remember climbing one. At best, they have the names of common trees like maple, apple, pine. Mostly, they call them trees. Trees have become an amorphous category without nuance. Rarely would a student bring me maple leaves or chestnuts from outside. And I know they have to step over them to get to my studio. Once, a student asked me, "Ms. Elza, what are those things sticking out of the ground called?"

In 2007, the *Oxford Junior Dictionary* dropped over forty common nature words, among them *acorn, adder, bluebell, dandelion, fern, heron, kingfisher, newt, otter* and *willow*. The reasoning? They were not being used enough by children to justify keeping them. They were replaced with words like *blog, broadband, bullet point, cut-and-paste, attachment* and *voice mail*. Aldo Leopold said it well in *A Sand County Almanac*: "Education, I fear, is learning to see one thing by going blind to another."[11] He refers to the natural world as giving an education and the creatures in it as being his teachers. He calls his dog his professor and his farm a textbook.

Children learn what we put in front of them, until they can make better choices. Many children are over scheduled and lacking the free-play time needed to grow and develop their imaginations, minds and bodies; sadly, in impoverished urban environments, kids are also often held hostage inside apartments with wall-to-wall carpets where they interact with flat screens more often than with people, in an environment hosting a proliferation of allergies, mental illnesses and conditions. It's not a secret that exposing young brains to technology in the first five years of their life is detrimental to brain development and bonding. Brain scans show underdeveloped and disorganized white matter in the language and literacy areas.[12] Playing computer games obsessively shows a reduction in the parts of the brain responsible for executive functions. The same is observed in people with substance use disorders.[13] We realize just how damaging such lifestyle and exposure are to a child's physical and mental well-being—not to mention the planet. We are slow to take action. These are not choices children make. Recently, I came across another study claiming that teaching students empathy improves their creativity.[14] Yes, but it is their creativity to begin with that builds empathy with the living world. So, what are we doing at school or at home that so successfully teaches them out of both?

That March after the pandemic lockdown, we moved teaching online and children have been further pushed into the containment of rooms, this time *forced* to sit in front of screens. Their tactile learning through and with nature kept shrinking and their relationships were limited and truncated. I have been teaching online since March 2020 and I can see the struggle at the other end with children and parents. I can also feel the detrimental effects it has had on my mind, my voice and my body. During the pandemic, I gave my students homework where they had to go find a tree they were attracted to, shake hands with the tree, sit under the tree and write a poem to the tree. These poems ended up getting published in the anthology *Worth More Growing: Youth Poets and Activists Pay Homage to Trees.*[15]

My first love was a tree. We met on a different continent, in Sofia. Don't get me wrong, there were boys and, oh, did they like me. But this was different. I walked out of Sofia University one day, upset, burning with the fire of being misunderstood over a spat with a colleague. I crossed the street to the park and plopped myself on a bench under a tree. Compelled to look up, I was instantly transported by the sunlight filtering through the vaulted crown. Tension perceptibly drained from my body. Peace washed over me as if some kind of healing had happened, some kind of balance—restored. My petty concerns paled away before a profound presence. As Annie Dillard put it in *Pilgrim at Tinker Creek*: "It was less like seeing than like being for the first time seen, knocked breathless by a powerful glance."[16] Love at first sight. I went on with my day lighter, transformed.

In *I and Thou,* Martin Buber says, "if will and grace are joined, as I contemplate a tree I am drawn into a relation, and the tree ceases to be an It."[17] I returned to my tree often during my university years. He never disappointed me. I call *it* a *he*. English has a poverty of pronouns that quickly deprive a living being of its life and animacy. I have resisted it for so long that when I heard Robin Wall Kimmerer offer us an alternative, I jumped with delight. In her important work to bridge traditional and scientific knowledge on plants, she speaks of a word in Anishinaabe used to address beings of the living Earth: Bemaadiziiaaki. Aki means "Earth." She offers the last part of that word, ki, to serve as a pronoun that honours the more-than-human world of living things: "ki to signify a being of the living Earth. Not *he* or *she*, but *ki*. So that when we speak of Sugar Maple, we say, 'Oh that beautiful tree, ki is giving us sap again this spring.' And we'll need a plural pronoun, too, for those Earth beings. Let's make that new pronoun *kin*." [18] Through these pronouns, she goes on to address birds and trees as relatives. I will embrace this pronoun ki here as I speak of my tree.

No matter the season or weather, ki had something to offer. I gave my tree a name. I was not wise enough to marry ki. I was restless, wanted to travel, to move around, to move away, and ki could not follow me. If I'm lucky, ki will be there when I next go back to visit.

Years later, this experience showed up in a poem, in the voice of a much younger version of myself.

in her silent presence I would whisper
when from the world withdrawn
in her leaves I wrapped my secrets small
and left them to the crows.

A dozen years ago, I had a memorable exchange with a tree on a third continent during a hike with my family in Capilano River Regional Park. We stopped by a brass plaque. The name of this massive, old-growth Douglas fir is Grandpa Capilano. Singled out, ki didn't look that different from the other trees in the area. I read the plaque to my seven-year-old son. Something about the distance in time—being a sprout at the time of Christopher Columbus (I wish there was a better point of reference)—something about the size of the tree (2.4 metres in diameter, 61 metres tall) or was it because the tree was called Grandpa (reminding me of our inherent, undeniable lineage and connection)—overwhelmed me. I encountered this ancient being in its all-at-once-ness and my voice cracked.

"What's wrong, Mama?" my son asked.

I didn't know what was wrong. I didn't know what was right either. I buried the puzzlement at the back of my head. Time passed and another poem sprouted. And I knew it was in response to that moment. An excerpt of the poem goes:

and you do not know how
you know it is not grief that fills
the eye with tears.[19]

I knew these tears were not grief. I wanted to know what they were. What was this overwhelming feeling? A beautiful thing, ever so brief. How much of our lives is spent elsewhere. These were tears of love. You cannot grieve that which you do not love. Was it also a recognition of coming home?

Words matter. Trees and humans share more than we can comprehend but let's begin with limbs, trunks, crowns, cells, verticality, roots, imagination using the same chemicals we have in our brains. *We are made and remade from the breath of trees* keeps echoing in my mind. How we name is how we remember. As if I have a memory of being ki once. As if we have shared the same *skin,* as if our cells remember the urgency of what is life giving, the life-force, ki, that connects us all. "Poetry is what I start to hear when I concede the world's ability to manage and to understand itself," says Robert Bringhurst in *The Tree of Meaning.*[20] No wonder I turned to poetry for my answers. To be fully present one has to succumb to something bigger than logic or reason. Poetry is an opening. In poetry, we can do something with words that words shouldn't be able to do. I can be a tree. We can be a forest together. Again, the powerful voice of Kimmerer rings in my mind:

> Language can be a tool for cultural transformation. Make no mistake: "ki" and "kin" are revolutionary pronouns. Words have power to shape our

> thoughts and our actions. On behalf of the living world, let us learn the grammar of animacy. We can keep "it" to speak of bulldozers and paperclips, but every time we say "ki," let our words reaffirm our respect and kinship with the more-than-human world. Let us speak of the beings of Earth as the "kin" they are.[21]

Imagine children's dictionaries adopting this pronoun? Children will understand more readily such an address since the world is still alive for them, before we reduce it and stop its breath with an *it*.

When we violate the ecosystems we are part of, our bodies grieve. It takes time for the mind to catch up, to rationalize this grief. I wish it didn't take so long to wake up to it. We are becoming more and more aware that this living world is something we can unravel and destroy. We now speak of ecological grief and it is so perceptible that we need a new word, *solastalgia*, to describe it. *Ecology* comes from the Greek word *oikos*, meaning "house." We are grieving the unravelling of our home. This is not something outside of us. Home that does not feel like home is an unravelling inside of us.

As I write this, we are still fighting against the logging of old-growth trees. My son spent a whole summer up at Fairy Creek defending old growth. The treatment they got from the special unit of police was despicable. I hate to think my taxes are going to such violence toward our young people, who will be inheriting the loss and the mess adults are making of their world. In Mexico, a group of women activists are getting married to trees to draw attention to illegal logging. In other parts of the world, people are fighting to give rivers the right of personhood. If a corporation can have such rights, why not a river or a forest or a mountain? Here in Canada, we are still filling out surveys and questionnaires to defend the rights of these ancient beings. They distract us with questions like, What does the phrase *old growth* mean to you? or, What are the top three reasons you feel old-growth forests are important? I'm not kidding. This is not a matter of perception. Just the other day, I filled out a survey in my province of British Columbia with such questions. As if we are in some grade four classroom just beginning to explore the topic. I suspect the questions are asked in a way that will angle the results to serve the decisions already made. Words matter. Are politicians shifting the label "old growth" now so that it does not include the mature original trees? In this upcoming election, I'll be talking to another politician about this and instead of a turkey for Thanksgiving, I will be roasting them with questions. The question "What does *old growth* mean to you?" does not seem benign anymore. How we label the animate world matters. How the meaning slips and shifts under our noses is significant. All this as the forests burn, as the cedars come down, as we keep digging up coal and gas and still subsidizing it like there is no tomorrow.

We found ourselves in the next predicament—the pandemic. A convenient distraction from the big issues but also a wonderful moment of pause where, if we were lucky, we had more time to examine the many ways we are failing people and planet. We argue and protest as if we need to convince anyone that we need clean water or air to survive. Our bodies are screaming at us to pay attention. The bigger the awareness and love for the planet, the bigger the grief. We are the children of the trees and our children are watching. If they look away, we fall.

In 2018, in protest of the omitted nature words from the dictionary, Robert Macfarlane and Jackie Morris wrote and illustrated a spell book that conjures back twenty of the missing words. *The Lost Words* has a poem dedicated to each word. It begins with summoning *acorn* back into the world and ends with *wren*. The book is big and impressive—about thirty-eight centimetres tall.[22] I have a copy in my office. My students peel the pages one at a time and think about the connection between a word and what it represents, between signifier and signified.

How do we re-wild the childhood imagination amidst all this devastation and impoverishment? In my class, I keep rocks, leaves, moss, twigs, pinecones and chestnuts. I have a bowl of beach rocks to which I add water. We admire how the rocks change colour when they get wet. This is our stone soup. We name the rocks and turn them into characters in stories. We inspire our senses to look longer, deeper, further. We read picture books by Indigenous and First Nations authors with Indigenous wisdom and research Indigenous plants and their properties. We write poems. We add to our reading list *Braiding Sweet Grass*, adapted for youth by Monique Gray Smith.[23] The braiding of Indigenous wisdom, scientific knowledge and the teaching of the plants is crucial to developing relationships with ki.

As adults, we are in danger of forgetting that we, too, need to nourish ourselves from the source. Being in touch with where life comes from is crucial in not depriving our children from it. Martin Buber tells us in *I and Thou* that the other does not fully come into being unless we form a loving relationship with *it*.[24] If he knew Kimmerer, he might have said: *a loving relationship with ki and kin*.

What a simple idea: love as methodology. It is how I treat my students, my children, people, animals, rocks and trees. It's hard to grieve that which you are not connected to in the first place. And you can only grieve if you have loved what is being lost. We have to model this to our kids.

When my older son was about seven, he drew a picture of... I could not tell what. Seashells?

He corrected me. "Tree stumps, Mama. See, the trees have burned."

Indeed, two red glowing dots, the eye of tree or root, underneath a mouth or scar, as if the earth was hurt. The third stump had wispy lines coming up from it, faint, like the memory of something gone.

"Look," he said, "and this is the spirit of the tree that has burned." He is turning twenty-seven this year and I do not have comfort for him that we are wiser. But I trust he is.

Again, I hear the scream of the saws and the rumbling of the shredders. They are back for the next batch of felled cedar. This is not a localized phenomenon. Cedars have been dying in the last few years with the dry summers. Too dry for cedar in cedar country. The trees come down. The words disappear from the dictionary and from children's minds. Not because children do not use them but because we do not find them important enough to keep and to teach. And so, species disappear on the edge of our inattention.

We spell and speak the names in class: acorn, adder, bluebell, dandelion, fern, heron, kingfisher, newt, otter, willow. We write poems to them. We write letters to the *Oxford Junior Dictionary* to bring them back.

Writer Anne Lamott says: "This business of becoming conscious… is ultimately about asking yourself… How alive am I willing to be."[25] We cannot truly be alive if we do not connect to where life comes from. Polish philosopher Henryk Skolimowski says, "life is a growing tree of sensitivities."[26] We are the ones that have to grow those sensitivity trees inside our minds first. We need these new tree organs to imagine the future.

Once regarded as you, or ki, the tree becomes a presence more than an object of investigation. In a 1997 interview titled "Listening with Courtesy," Tim Lilburn added to my hope with the following stance. I ran with it even though Lilburn didn't sound too optimistic at the time. He said:

> There's consciousness as thief, going in to this thing that is not it and taking stuff out; there's consciousness as stranger, never on the inside. But if this possibility is true there is consciousness as integral or necessary to the thing, partici-

> patory. Eros becomes part of cosmology: the tree in order to be this tree and no other tree needs me or you or somebody else to need it, love it, celebrate it. Then it becomes itself in the excitement of human consciousness.[27]

I have been obsessed with this kind of eros ever since. We have even diminished eros over the centuries. Limited it to ourselves and our bodily pursuit. How human of us. There is an ecstasy in transcending yourself, in leaving our small ego-driven worlds, in standing outside and beside yourself. To connect and relax in the arms of something much more expansive and nourishing seems like a luxury. It is not. It is a necessity. I dare you to try it. The world looks different under trees.

I visited my first love a few years ago. Ki was hard to find. I'd forgotten the details of ki's features. I didn't know what state ki was in. I was worried ki might have gotten sick, might've been taken down like the cedars. The place had changed. We cannot sit still like trees, we are not satisfied, we constantly alter the world to feel like we are doing something, to feel alive. As children of the trees, what do we owe the trees? They give to us so generously.

And there ki was. It was not a sunny day so I couldn't see the sunlight through ki's massive crown. I sat underneath quietly until I felt ki, too, remembered me. We sat like that for a long time. I told ki this story. I told ki about the next three rusty cedars looking at me through my window. Marked with big orange dots, they are slated to be chopped and shredded. And I was not sure how to comfort ki.

A Kaleidoscope of Childhood

My sister and I sit back to back on the floor of our room in Sofia, Bulgaria. We speak gibberish, pretend it's the new language we are going to learn because no one will speak the one we understand. I'm seven. She is four. We spend hours enunciating made up words with unfamiliar intonation. We pretend we know what we are saying. We're told the new country will be very hot and we'll be there for only two years.

We lived in Nigeria much longer than that. We grew up there.

:first day of school:

I don't speak a word of English, copy letters painstakingly from the blackboard. My classroom has dark green metal shutters for windows. On the first day of school, the only thing I can do is draw. I draw Snow White and the seven dwarfs. Not at work but at play. One of the dwarfs is swinging from a branch. My classmates crowd around me, point to different parts of my picture, then put their notebooks in front of me so I draw in their books too. The girls trace the blue veins on my arms, want to braid my hair. I let them.

They say if you remember something, you change it. They say if you want to keep it pure, you do not remember it.

The first book assigned by my teacher is *Mr. Happy*. At recess, I eat what the other kids eat even though my parents said not to eat anything we did not bring to school. We take off our shoes, too, run around barefoot. The school compound is mostly sand. We learn to sing a song in Hausa.

Zo zo zo,
zo abokina,
zo mutafi makaranta.

The song is all about going to school. At night, after the heat subsides, I sit on the veranda and learn *Mr. Happy* by heart.

:new house:

While we wait for our house to be built, we live in a guest house bungalow. It's like a hotel but with tiny houses instead of rooms. My sister and I have little flashlights to light our way at night so we don't step on something poisonous like a scorpion or snake. In the restaurant, I have porridge for the first time. There are also eggs, sausages and kidneys for breakfast. I learn how to ask for water in English. I look at the kidneys for a long time before going back to my seat.

We're robbed within the first week of moving into our new house. The thieves even take our curtains and freshly roasted peanuts we left on the dining room table. They leave the chess set behind, carefully propped on the edge of a drawer. The chess pieces, which roll noisily around in the wooden box, must have tried to sound the alarm. The next day, we have bars put on our windows.

Memories arrive. Permeable membranes I move through with recognition. I find there more than I thought I would.

:playground:

Past the shade of the tamarind tree in the backyard is a wide riverbed. The other side is where the out-of-bounds bush begins. My sister and I are not allowed to go there. Sometimes, the waters trickle in streams on the riverbed. Sometimes, we find mussel shells. They look like the eyes of dangerous beasts. Did they come from the ocean this far north? This is our riverbed, our afternoon school, our playground. We never saw the riverbed fill up.

I get a kaleidoscope and a doll on New Year's Eve. Also a wide-brimmed purple hat. I see my first snake while hanging upside down on the swing. The next snake I see is a cobra with something dead, or dying, in its mouth. Someone said they once found a snake curled up in their bed. For months, I look under my covers before getting into bed.

:Mr. Happy:

I'm very upset with my dad. I run away from home for the first time. I leave *Mr. Happy* behind and walk all the way to the edge of the compound. Lines from *Mr. Happy* run through my head: *On the other side of the world where the sun shines hotter than here,* it begins. That's impossible. Nothing can be hotter than here. And I came from the other side of the world, left the trees that were *a hundred feet tall* and all my friends. I sit on the curb behind the green hedge and wait. And wait. It feels like forever. No one comes to look for me. I walk back home. No one noticed I was gone.

Each remembered moment blooms in the present. Each moment brings me home. A turn of the kaleidoscope spins under the growing light of my attention. I am now an immigrant here. I sit on the curb and wait.

:milk:

My best friend, Helhara, and I walk with our empty bottles and kobo coins to where we wait till the cows come home, and the bulls. I don't like the bulls, they charge. Kids from the nearby village are already here. We play while we wait. We suck on tamarind. That's our candy. We keep passing a baby around. We have to look after her. When it's my turn, I hold her as if she is something I might break. She holds tight as if she is attached to my hip. Her skin is velvety as if she has no bones in her soft body. She giggles, grips my clothes. She has to. We're playing tag.

The distance stirs with dust. The herd moves slowly across the endless yellow savannah. A flame tree here, a baobab there break the flat horizon. We watch the bulls closely, stay near the oil drums so we can duck for cover. We line up and wait for the herdsman to milk the cows. The milk froths in the bucket. I give him my sweaty kobo coins, he fills my green glass bottle.

It's instantly warm in my hands. Sometimes, the milk is not enough for everyone.

I bring the neighbour's toddler home. She has on the tiniest straw hat. When she sees my parents, she cries and cries as if she has seen ghosts.

A memory is suddenly there. We do something with it. I don't want the misguided hands or dirty fingerprints of others all over my childhood.

My parents grow things. My dad is in charge of big mango orchards that grow every kind of mango and he has to walk around big farms of tomatoes and hot and sweet peppers and probably okra (which gets gooey when you cook it but, oh, so delicious in a stew). He helps the farmers collect seeds for the next season. People ask me what my parents do and I don't know what to say. The farms and orchards are so big and so many. A few words will not describe the variety and taste of those mangoes. Alphonso and Peter are just two of the varieties. My dad's name is Peter. For a while, I thought that was the name for the mangoes he grew and they were named after him. It's like my kaleidoscope, each turn is unique and there is no description to make up for it. So, I just say: *They grow things*.

:garden:

In our garden, we grow tomatoes, peppers, okra, eggplant, *yakuwa, alaiyaho*, melons, corn and groundnuts. There is so much mint in the shade around the garden tap. My sister and I are in charge of the radishes, the carrots and the lettuce. We thin them out, weed and water them. When I'm older, I take care of the chickens. We even have a patch of banana trees, a mango tree, a cashew tree and a few guava trees. Helhara laughs when she sees me eat guava for the first time. She shows me how to not spit out all the tiny seeds.

Are memories seeds? My childhood happened on its own continent, with its own climate. I've been away for so long. Sometimes, I am afraid to remember not to tarnish the memory.

My sister watches my dad pick watermelons: he taps, listens, then cuts the stem. She does the same: taps, listen, cuts the stem. She picks all the melons, even the green ones. She's very proud of herself. She's not allowed to go near the watermelon patch for weeks.

:rainstorm:

Often in the rainy season, the sky turns twilight orange at midday. Everything looks strange in the tinted light. I can smell the thin dust in the air, the storm that is brewing. We go in and pull back the curtains. I'm mesmerized by the deafening thunder, the forked lightning. We count in the in-betweens. The wind picks up and toys with trees, bending their backs as far as they will go.

At night, each time lightning strikes we see a different picture, each tree in a different pose. I cannot focus on anything during a rainstorm. Forget the show on the small black-and-white TV, forget the math homework, there's a storm brewing outside and this show only lasts for a few minutes. A tree in the backyard once snapped in half. One of its branches went right through our roof.

Moments come in like lightning flashes, brief and quick. They freeze in the frame. When they dissipate, the world is clearer, more resolute, the contours sharper after the rain.

Sometimes, the storm is so bad it topples power lines. One year, we didn't have electricity for three months. Or what felt like three months. The fridge was just another cupboard. My dad hooked up our tiny TV to the car battery so we could watch our favourite cartoons on the hood of the car. My mom cooked on the fire outside. The food was more delicious.

These are nothing like my memories from the two other continents I lived on. A part of me remains there inside a carefully woven cocoon. How to make first contact with what is fragile, dreaming, susceptible to mutation? I don't want it interpreted.

Another time, a storm levels all our corn flat to the ground during the night. When I see it in the morning, I cry. The plants are only as tall as we are. My sister and I, secretly, spend the day propping up each plant, hundreds of them. When our parents come home from work, all the corn is standing up. That night, the two of us are so proud. We are also itchy from where the corn plants touched our skin. We cannot sit still.

:the harmattan:

When the winds change direction, the Sahara Desert comes to visit. It hangs in the air, blurs the houses, the distances, the trees. It's the uninvited guest. It sneaks in like a thief. You can't keep it out of your house. I cannot sleep from the dusty smell. My mom makes me a gauze mask, wets it, puts it on my face at night. In the morning, everything is covered in the fine red dust. My sister and I draw and write secret messages to each other on the dining room table before my mom shines it clean for breakfast.

How to make contact with what becomes suspicious of itself? Fine dust settles after a memory.

Two streets down, my friend's house gets robbed. He tries to help his dad fight off the robbers. You never fight the robbers. They are never alone. He is stabbed more than once. I cannot believe the news.

When he is better, he comes over to my house. I cannot keep my eyes off the star-like scar left after the wound in his chest heals. Even when he comes over the next time. And the time after.

I write these flashes down at first contact to protect them from even my own judgement. An altar of many icons. A time capsule that consumes me with wonder after the seal is broken. I keep them in their fragile shells, afraid of what would hatch if I speak them.

In high school, I learn to wear the *wrappa*. It's a rectangular cloth that wraps around my legs all the way down to my ankles. Two strings secure it around my waist. It's the bottom half of my uniform. I can only make small steps to get anywhere. It feels strange for a piece of cloth to restrain my wide stride so much. At recess, I pull up the *wrappa* to my knees and run.

:heat:

The neighbours are burning the grass in their yard. Flames creep to the edge of our yard. Our corn is ripe and ready for picking; it has that dry-rustle sound. The corn is all around our house. My sister and I are alone at home. If the corn catches on fire, the house might too. Fire alarms sound in our little heads. We snap low-hanging branches off neem trees and stand between the fire and the corn. Our neem brooms beat down any little flame that jumps or sneaks past the fence. We're hot, itchy, scared and covered in soot. My dad is so upset when he gets home, scolds us for putting ourselves in danger. Later, we are heroes for saving the corn and maybe even the house.

I hang the laundry outside on the clothesline in our yard. By the time I'm done, the first thing I pinned up is already dry. On such days, I stay in the shade, I don't want to go out until dusk. It's hard to imagine there might be a place hotter than here. I'm now sixteen. I wonder where *Ms. Happy* lives and why she does not have a book of her own. Snow White is too hard to think about now. I go through book after book of *Jack and the Beanstalk* to find out if any of them gave the giant's wife a name. I write a book where I name her and I hear her thoughts.

At the end of the day, the sky is a brush of rose. The sound of drumming in the distance. Sometimes, the sunset is an orange ball slowly sinking out of sight. A peace descends as if the world has settled all its fights for the day, is hushed at the sight of the dying light. I forget to garden, stare into the distance, get carried away on the twilight. The garden prepares its beds for the night.

I hear a slight tapping on the shell that separates a memory from the world. A small whirlwind of leaves landing. Ghostly drums at sunset. Lightning in a thunderstorm at night. A glimpse of the trees frozen, just like this, in the flash. Then, it's dark again.

Turning Inside Out

I never thought I had a body to be proud of. In my mind, my legs were stubby and short, my hips too wide, my thighs and arms too full. Each year in high school, the nurse would record our weight and height. I was always 159 and a half centimetres. Each year, I waited to be 160 centimetres. Sheer willpower wasn't going to make me taller. When I got older and became aware that even my buttocks were the target of a guy's gaze, it felt like it dragged behind me on the ground like luggage. This wasn't how I wanted to feel. I might have been happy with average. But there was nothing average about me. I felt shorted on what being a woman meant, how she should look or behave. As a child, I was unaware of most of these things. Then we began to compare ourselves to each other.

I often butted heads with my dad on how he talked to my mom about her size and weight. Many fights with him were over comments he would make to her. I intuited he might have such expectations of me too. My mom had learned how to ignore him. She picked her battles. I was not so wise. I was also upset with her for putting up with that, for not fighting back. So, I fought harder. When my dad said I couldn't do something, I did it just to prove him wrong. He didn't like being wrong. When he commented on my body, it stuck to me like burrs.

He has a bad case of patriarchy refusing to die. I want to tell him all this. I want to open this tough nut for discussion, to crack it open the way he used to crack freshly picked walnuts in my grandmother's yard when I was little and feed their milky flesh to me under the ancient walnut tree. But now, I hold back. Those green walnut skins left brown stains on our hands for a long time. He is too fragile now for confrontation. I might not have enough time for such a stain to go away.

In my teens, not only did a lot of boys like me, they liked me a lot. I was bubbly, happy-go-lucky, bright-eyed and full of hope. I had bouncy blonde-auburn curls, hair that streaked and bleached in the summer, shone and shimmered. No dye could compete with such natural vitality. It felt like the outward expression of my inner vivaciousness and wilderness. My hair still feels like it is an expression of my poetry. People recognize me by my hair. My grandmother told me I had beautiful eyes; she said when I smiled, my eyes smiled too. I knew I had power over boys and I liked to use it. I liked their attention.

Feeling that power made me take liberties I regretted sometimes. I got into fights on the playground and thought I would get away easy. I was feisty, determined and stubborn. Boys mostly held back, perhaps due to sheer bafflement. They were taught not to hit girls. But occasionally, I ended up having to hold my end of a fight. In grade eight, a boy named Angel slapped me right back when I slapped him for saying something mean to me. Another boy I liked punched me back in the solar plexus so hard I thought I might never be able to take a breath again. I still preferred to hang out with boys. Most girls were boring to me, except my few best girlfriends with whom anything was possible. Dolls, clothes, fashion, bodies and boys weren't topics of interest. I didn't need to dwell on how my body was not up to "the standard" or look at painfully skinny models whose thighs didn't meet anywhere or whose thighs were as thick as my upper arms. As if we knew what a boy liked. Girls were falling under the spell of advertising, movies and fashion magazines. I was more interested in the big questions, my plus-sized thoughts, my budding teen philosophy, and I liked to be admired. Boys were fun. They played, they did adventurous and daring things like kicking a ball, climbing trees or stealing low-hanging fruit. It was a relief not to compare myself to yet another girl, or picture of a girl, or pretend I was interested in photos of guys in magazines. Every time a friend went gaga over some guy's photo, I said he probably isn't kind, smart or fun. That never went down well. It burst their bubble. Sadly, boys at that time were interested in a few things and those were mostly on my blooming body.

In Nigeria, when I was sixteen, a Hungarian man had a crush on me. He was twenty-four. Our families were friends. To take me out to a party, he had to ask permission from my dad. My dad liked that. It was something he knew and it was the way things were supposed to be in his world, or in the movies we watched. Although when there was kissing and other more intimate scenes on TV, my dad would go to the kitchen to get water or a snack of freshly roasted groundnuts from the garden and conveniently come back when it was over.

This was going to be my first official date. I was excited to be asked but annoyed that my dad had to be involved in this transaction. I had no autonomy to leave the house on my own, in a place where you only get where you want to go by driving or being driven. I also knew it wasn't going to be a game of Scrabble. I was good at that and had won a number of times when he'd come over for a visit. I was mostly bored at the party and felt like I was on display, which probably meant I didn't fit in. Did I wear the wrong clothes? I hated my clothes. I felt like Maria in *The Sound of Music*. My skirt was made of material my mother made curtains with. But what beautiful and delicate curtains those were. I made that skirt and was proud of it. Perhaps I stood out because of the things I said? On the way back from the party, we stopped on the side of the road, which was dangerous to do in Maiduguri. He kissed me. He asked me what I would do with my hands and my hands immediately felt like dead birds in my lap. What was wrong with me?

When I went back to Bulgaria, I didn't know I was going through a culture shock in (what I thought was) my own country. But it wasn't my country anymore. I hadn't lived there for ten formative years. My childhood friends were teenagers who spoke a language I didn't fully understand. How to join in the lingo and activities of my peers? All these tug-of-wars reflected in my body. I stayed home a lot, shut myself in my room. I sang songs from *The Sound of Music* (I did like Maria a lot) and songs from other musicals. They gave me comfort. I gained extra kilos. I didn't know how to dress for parties. My ideas of what would look good on me and what actually looked good on me were on racetracks that didn't meet. I couldn't afford the clothes I wanted and the ones I wore were likely not well suited nor the right size for my body. The whole fashion game wasn't on my radar at first and later, I refused to play it.

I was bombarded with all sorts of images and ads for what the perfect body looked like. The idea of all-night parties where people smoked and got drunk, where I was one of the few the next day who remembered what happened, didn't appeal for long. I felt foreign, an outsider in what should've been my country. (My friends later told me I sounded funny when I spoke Bulgarian with an English accent.) There were two categories of women: sluts and virgins, à la *Grease*. I was thrown constantly between these extremes that were also on their separate tracks. You couldn't be both. What was the right way for a girl to be in this new context? What was right for her to do, and how, with a boy? Am I slutty if I let a boy kiss me? What if I'm naked with a boy? I remember asking my mother once in exasperation, "Mom, how do you know when you are in love?"

She paused for a moment and said, "You'll know."

So, I waited for the moment I would know—as if that would protect me somehow.

In hindsight, those extra kilos were both a blessing and a curse. They were a protection between me and the world, a kind of blubber that kept me from being liked too much or taken advantage of. Was I trying to hide in there? It didn't help that I grew up between continents and felt alien and strange. Food became more of a comfort. I was addicted to these herby cheese puffs when I studied for exams. I bit my nails. I wore clothes that were ill-fitting to hide all I thought was wrong with me.

For a while, I got into sewing. I sewed things on my mom's hand-crank sewing machine. I liked what I sewed. It looked good on me and complemented my shapes and curves. I didn't feel at odds with my body when I wore the successful outcomes. It was a creative outlet, like writing, which my parents were also worried about.

The pressure on a girl at university was immense. It was stressful enough in high school. There were students who were getting married. Some had kids and some were already contemplating separations or divorce. The idea that there was something wrong with you if you were still a virgin seemed rampant. If you were poor, it was your fault. If you were a virgin, it was your fault. As if it was something to be ashamed of. Martin liked me a lot but also acted like many women liked him. He acted like he was a super popular guy. And maybe he was but that wasn't what was going to attract me to him. I don't know why that should ever be a good reason.

One lunch break, we were sitting in the sunshine on the steps of the university between the two huge statues of Evlogi and Hristo Georgiev that frame the grand entrance to Sofia University. They were the brothers who helped finance the building of the university. Dressed in suits, looking official, comfortably seated, they looked like they were checking out anyone who came in or out. Martin, as usual, dropped his hint of when were he and I going to… I laughed it off as I always did. As we talked and flirted between the stone men, he told me there was a saying: *If a woman graduates from Sofia University a virgin, these two statues will stand up*.

"Are you saying no one graduates a virgin?" I asked. Then, without missing a beat, "Are you charged with the burden of making sure they never stand up?" I did not easily succumb to peer pressure. But it was never a comfortable feeling. This whole are-you-still-a-virgin thing remained, haunted me. I also wanted to unsettle the statues and make them stand up, prove Martin wrong.

There were all sorts of moments in which I could truly have been in harm's way and I was both cautious and oblivious to them at the same time. Often, due to sheer intuition and wit, I managed to get myself out of crappy or potentially dangerous situations. When walking home at night, I had my leather purse wrapped around my hand, ready to swing it at any moment. It helped that I didn't drink. The only time I did get drunk was due to a silly bet I made at a party when I was about seventeen.

"I bet you cannot drink this," says a guy swirling a glass of cognac.

"Sure, I can," I say without thinking.

Thankfully, I was in my best friend's apartment. I spent the rest of that New Year's Eve face down on her bed. My head felt like a rock tumbler with rocks grinding around each time I moved. I'd look out the window at the floating balconies on the building across hoping the balconies would slip back into their proper slots. I even missed the moment my best friend's hair caught on fire during the countdown when someone held a sparkler too close to her heavily sprayed hair.

Then there was the journalist who was quite a few years older and did not hide his admiration, even though he was married and had a kid. I had fun with him and was enamoured. Older men really liking me was becoming a pattern and I liked the fact that I could talk to them while I was waiting for my peers to grow up. One night, we were coming back from a party on the outskirts of town and the buses had stopped running. He suggested we sleep at his office nearby. I was fine with that—him being married and all—until I realized there was one bed and we were both going to sleep in it. I didn't take my clothes off. He was eager and excited. I turned away from him. He was insistent. I looked at him straight in the eye and said, "Okay, we'll do it, and... so what?" On the inside I was petrified but that phrase worked like magic. He turned away, plopped on the bed disgruntled and fell asleep. It might not have turned out so well.

The nature of the work I did at the time as a translator and interpreter meant I often travelled with the people I was interpreting for, spending long days and evenings with them. I received a lot of apologies from men whose advances were not met with the expected enthusiasm from sober me. While I was flirting with ideas, they thought I was flirting with them. I had to be diplomatic while I also stood my ground. I made sure I was never the one who had to apologize the next day—and that required having good boundaries. (My mom's words often ran through my head: *Never lift your skirt where you work.* I thought that was crass coming from my sweet mom but it seemed to do the job.) A charming fifty-year-old man thought I was fair game one night but I tactfully staved off his advances. The next morning, he knocked on my door while I was getting dressed, profusely apologizing before the day's work began. The first snow of the year had started falling. I poked my head, hiding behind the door, and surprised myself by saying to him: "You can't blame the snow for falling." I was angry but how do you say what you think, keep your job and stay safe?

My body image didn't change much in my twenties. I was a no-bare-arms and no-bare-legs kind of girl. To this day, I do not remember my size in clothes since it changed each time and with each brand. Moving countries also changed how clothes were sized but I was also sure the industry was playing mind games with me. And then, there were my hips. Each time I found something that worked, it would get discontinued. I still get a measurement each time I shop for bras. If guys found me attractive and desirable, why was I still not feeling good about my body? Was it because I thought they were mostly desperate? I wished I had given myself more credit.

❦

After I got married, my husband reminded me how I wore a sweater to hide my hips and curves when we met. He liked what I was hiding under that big sweater. He must've told me he liked me enough times that it began to change how I felt. I also realized he called me *honey* only if some criticism was about to follow. That was the end of *honey*. Now, I also knew I wasn't a virgin anymore. I considered myself a virgin until I met the guy who cared enough to give me my first orgasm. That was when I felt different. The first time I had intercourse was a baffling, dull kind of experience. I thought it was hyped up way too much for what it delivered.

The only time I didn't worry about my body was when I didn't have time. Raising kids was a whirlwind. I needed time to myself. I often forgot to eat. Writing seemed to satiate me. It kept me busy thinking about things other than myself. Also, I had to work, shop, plan meals and cook for my family. When I could, I stayed away from the kitchen as much as possible. It was a chore to even get lunch for myself. My body didn't feel like it was my business card anymore.

No diet helped me because a diet just took something away. In hindsight, what worked was changing how I thought of food and how I thought of myself too. It happened when I began to reinstate activities that satiated the small voids that had formed inside of me. Writing, yoga and community filled growing holes life was digging for me. I latched onto them out of necessity. They reminded me what sanity felt like. And sanity can be addictive. I considered writing my happy place, my addiction. Some didn't like me saying that, arguing that addictions are destructive. But I knew better. I craved my quiet time like a drug and when I did not get it, I was a worse version of myself. These thoughts and activities replaced the ones that were eating me on the inside. It was when one of my best friends chose a sleeveless dress for me to wear and told me I looked good in it that I bared my arms and I even started wearing shorter skirts.

There were other bodies around me now that I had to take care of and worry about. My kids loved attention, loved hugs and kisses. They needed care to stay healthy, to feel beautiful and be fit. My five year old planted a kiss on my lips once while visiting my parents. They were taken aback and said I shouldn't let him do that. A reprimand from my dad? I told him every child needs to be loved, kissed and hugged. My son gets what he needs at five. Who helps kids feel good about their bodies? Where better to begin than at home? The gaze of a parent is defining.

I refused to stop hugging my boys and planting kisses on their beautiful faces. If a father doesn't hug them, if their mother doesn't hug them or kiss them, then who would? Too often, men don't know how to hold a woman. For many, the feeling of intimacy is lost in the sex act. Why leave it to the porn industry and the dry sex Ed classes in school for them to figure out how to navigate intimacy and love? They taught them nothing about love in school under the pretext that it's not something you could teach. A lot has been said and written about love. My kids were also learning from how we attended to our bodies daily. They began to be bombarded with judgements and questions about their own bodies.

"Mom, why is everyone in my class a head taller than me?" one of my sons asked.

"You are as tall as you need to be," I replied. "Your feet reach the ground, don't they?"

That baffled them and we would laugh it off. I am glad my kids weren't fashion freaks and weren't easily susceptible to peer pressure either. I cannot imagine what life would be like if I had to spend time at the malls in service of the next fashion trend. I avoid malls with a vengeance. I only have about a thirty-minute tolerance for shopping.

I regret to say that it's only recently, as I got closer to fifty, that I really began to like my body. I regret that it took so long, that for most of my life, my body and how I felt about it were defined by others, by how people looked at me, how advertisers advertised to me. How I feel about myself changed from the inside out. I walk taller, I feel beautiful and I take nothing short of adoration from men. Food is something to savour and sustain, not to use as distraction. It's an aesthetic experience that sustains physiologically and psychologically. I avoid eating when too busy; otherwise, I'm unlikely to remember what I ate. I give myself time in the evening to devour my one main meal with delight and feel the luxury in each bite. My grandmother was right: *Chew every bite thirty-two times,* she would often say. I've never counted but it feels close. My doctor tells me I should eat more often, but how to secure that space in this busy tornado of a life I live? I'm the same way in my relationships. Quality is better than quantity. Candlelight, wine and conversations; phones and computer screens banished to another room. We define so much of each other just by the way we attend to each other, the way we look at each other. I am wary of people's gaze.

I am a plus-sized woman but not the way it is usually thought of. I am too big for my body. My thought body and my spiritual body have grown out of the boundaries of my physical body. Perhaps I always felt that discrepancy. It took me a long time to realize I don't need a big body to house that. I pick the corner seats, go for the aisle or window seats. I'm too big to sit in the centre of a row in the theatre. I feel others pressing on me with their emotions and stresses, which follow me home. I cannot watch horror movies. It hurts. The world is frightening enough. Violence shouldn't be entertainment.

I'm too much to handle but not in the way I used to think. I'm often too big for a small-minded world. I'm still waiting for some of my peers to grow up. I keep joking gossip gives me a rash but it turns out that wasn't a joke. My skin responds to psychological turmoil—it burns or itches. I'm too big for pettiness, for stuffy and snobby rooms and conversations. I realized it is okay to spill out of my body, it's okay to be bigger in many ways the world cannot handle but desperately needs. The world sure is taking its time to catch up. I'm not ashamed of it anymore. And I know I'm not the only one.

What Do You Do Again?

There's a sense of guilt that comes with doing work you are not paid for, be it full-time parenting, volunteering or writing. I've done all of these, at the same time. Plagued by the fact I wasn't making money, I tried to get all the housework done, to be fully dedicated to what my kids needed and to be a fun-to-work-with volunteer. If there was time to get to my writing, I'd get to it. The strategy backfired miserably—housework was never done, the kids took all the attention I gave them and the volunteer work multiplied. At the end of the day, right about when my husband came home from his work—a paid job—I was a wreck. I had spent the day running myself into the ground and collapsed into a pile of tears.

I was caught in a vicious cycle: I didn't make money parenting or volunteering so I didn't think I deserved the time to write. I had moved countries, left friends behind, moved away from a doctoral program and wasn't giving myself time to do what I loved. I had abandoned what I lived for. Except for my kids, of course. I was fully dedicated to them. That's what was wrong with me. I had abandoned my bigger dreams. I had nothing left to give at the end of the day. My husband probably thought he'd married one of Picasso's weeping women.

For years, I sent my parents stacks of poems. Silence followed. I worried they didn't "get" my poems, written in a language not their own. They can function in English but it is far from their Bulgarian mother tongue. It turned out they weren't convinced that's how I should be spending my time. They were the ones that surrounded us with beauty and poetry; why was that *not* desirable? There was tension between us for decades about what their now-adult offspring should be doing. Their mantra was: finish your doctorate, get a job. A job meant work with a pension plan. I did finish my doctorate. A pension plan was harder to get. The fact that pension plan jobs have been eroding for the last few decades was even harder to get through to them. I had no ground to stand on while trying to shift the margins on what was useful, important or necessary work.

It hurt more when I could not get that message through to family, friends and others near or dear to me. My identity and worth in the world seemed to be mostly defined by jobs that paid and, preferably, paid well. Still, my physical and spiritual multi-tasking was purposeful, my productivity was joyful and my life was infused with meaning. Writing brought me daily delights and well-being. I was taking a risk banking on this attitude and was often made to feel a failure. On the other hand, friends with well-paying jobs envied me and wanted to give up their jobs to remember that sense of having purpose, to remember what meaningful and creative work felt like.

Years ago, my kids wanted pets. I had two rules: it shouldn't shed and it shouldn't eat live things. It took me a month to get over the baby rats they brought home. The other choice was a snake. I grew up in Nigeria where snakes are not pets. The very word in Bulgarian for rat (Плъх, pronounced *pluh*) shares a root with the word for fear.

Those cuddly baby rats fit perfectly in my children's palms. The patience, care and attention they lavished on them over time changed how I felt. Love like that is contagious. After a while, rats didn't seem so bad. One day I told a neighbour in my housing co-operative that we had rats. A blend of horror and *I'm sorry* spun through her eyes and landed on her face. It took me a minute to realize that I had forgotten to qualify the rats as pets. I'd seen that look before. It is the look I get when I admit to being a poet.

After years of mentoring, teaching and building community and publishing six books, I still feel that to get the world's recognition I have to have a "real" job. Then, perhaps I'd get the stamp of approval from my parents. Maybe even from my husband's family. His sister nonchalantly once referred to him as my sugar daddy, salt on an already open wound. It reinforced that what I did wasn't seen as work even by the people closest to me, be it parenting, writing, volunteering at my kids' school, my housing co-op or in literary organizations. But she has cats, not kids.

Volunteer work is the fuel on which many writing organizations, reading series and literary journals run. The good kind of fuel, one that doesn't cause lasting damage to ecosystems. The kind of oil you want to spill and share. What would schools do without fundraising or parent volunteers? Committed to raising decent humans, I believe looking after my sons is the most important job I might ever do. It also is the hardest. The work we do in our co-op housing complex builds social capital that does not show on the bottom line of spreadsheets. In the last few years, as a community, we have been focussing on renewing our lease with the City of Vancouver. This year, I will be on the board on top of the committees I already serve on. In a place with a deepening housing crisis, we provide truly affordable housing for those who cannot take part in the property market, for those who do not want to be slaves to property, for those who choose social equity over financial windfalls, for those who value living in a community and sharing the work to make it lighter. Keeping our rent affordable in Vancouver is gaining the status of an essential service in a city that has been building unaffordable housing for decades.

Still, this work doesn't look good when I go to open a bank account. Even my children were puzzled how to describe their mother's profession on those pesky school forms. I can't blame them. They were unlikely to see me write. I did that when they were not around. They rarely saw me perform. I did that in the evening when their dad put them to bed. I didn't have a designated office or employer. The bank had a hard time with that too. When I'm too exhausted to defend what I do, I just say: *I teach*.

What was even harder work during the years my sons were in school was to help them get through it. Between the underfunding of their classrooms and the growing apathy of their peers, it was a challenge to preserve their love for learning and verve for exploration. I sent them to school as whole beings and they came back in pieces I had to put together again before morning. I was at least well trained, being someone who had to do that for herself a lot. It was depleting to worry about what school was doing to their healthy minds and spirits. My older son summed it up nicely: "School interferes with my learning." I laughed out loud. When my younger son got to high school, he said: "Mom, the weekend is not enough to recover from school." He is the one that does not say a lot but when he does, he is accurate and insightful. I worked hard on keeping them happy when they weren't in school—support work that needed to be done, and well worth it.

In time, it dawned on me that all the jobs I did not only had little or no pay attached to them but also no immediate rewards. Parenting is hard work that people assume you will do well. Writing is hard work that takes years before you know if you're successful. It takes lots of trust. You have to believe in yourself when no one else does. By the time a book comes out, you're working on the next project or two. With teaching, it could be years before you reap the fruits of your labour. More likely, you'll never find out the difference you've made in someone's life. Delayed reward was what I had to get used to. There's both a beauty and pain to insight. The good news is the guilt diminishes with the insight.

After two decades of putting pen to paper, things haven't improved much on the financial *affront* for writers. In 2018, the Writers' Union of Canada conducted a survey. I filled it out. Over 85 percent of Canadian writers were falling below the poverty line at under $10,000 a year, likely less than the year before. In the previous three years alone, writers' compensation had fallen nearly 30 percent. Since 1998, writers' income has dropped by 78 percent.[28] The verdict was in: most writers need a day job to fund the endless hours they pour into their writing job. The pandemic did not improve our plight, though it was great to see writing organizations step up, get creative and offer more opportunities. The pandemic opened up much needed conversations around work. Many began rethinking their relationship to work and the effect it has on family and mental health. For decades, we have been told that our lives will improve with technological advancement and we have not seen any of that "trickle down" with the implementation of AI technologies. If anything, the heavy reliance on technology to get basic things done gives me more work. I now have to do a lot of work just to *get* to my work.

Whatever money I got from writing and teaching I jokingly called the ice cream money. My husband brought home the bread and bacon and I brought home the ice cream. Perhaps his sister was wrong with her flippant remark. Perhaps I was the sugar mommy.

After twenty years in a marriage, my husband and I separated. Suddenly, I needed to pay for more than ice cream and had to find more reliable sources of income. There's a lot of comfort in not having to worry when the next paycheque will come. I cut back on volunteer work and substituted it with poorly paid teaching work with no benefits. With two master's degrees and a doctorate, I discovered I am overqualified for most jobs. And in the teacher shortages we have, I am not even qualified to teach in public school? Seriously?

I still have to work three times as hard for my freelance work. When I made that statement in front of my boss in praise of a regular paycheque, he frowned. He thought I would only put a third of the effort at the job he hired me for. I had to clarify that what I meant was that finding the work, doing the work and making sure I get paid for the work amounts to 300 percent effort. I assured him I put a minimum of 110 percent in my work regardless.

A study conducted in British Columbia in 2023 on precarious work showed that "only 49 percent of workers surveyed had full-time, permanent jobs with benefits. The other half experienced various levels of insecurity, including contracts that were temporary, part-time, didn't offer dependable hours or lacked benefits."[29] I fell into that 51 percent category.

How do we shift the lens on what's worth paying for? Even the work to defend our right to get paid is done on volunteer time. Fighting the city for affordable housing is work my city government should be doing on my behalf but I suspect we are paying them their salaries to cheat us out of our non-profit housing co-operative, now that the land leases are expiring and developers are drooling over this "city-owned" waterfront. The city should not be wearing two hats. The city should not be acting like another landlord. This puts the city in a conflict-of-interest position. Is the city being a responsible landlord? Is it embracing its role of stewardship or just sale-ship? So, it falls on the shoulders of those already struggling to make ends meet to fight for their rights.

When people call me on the phone for donations to this or that charity or cause, I tell them I'm a writer, most of the work I do is charity work. There is an awkward silence at the other end of the line. My sense of humour has also improved. How else can I talk about such unfunny things. Humour is one of my survival tools. I do the work I do not because I am into suffering but because I believe it is important work. My parents recently phrased it as: *You've picked a hard life for yourself*. That's an upgrade from before, when they told me *I was wasting my life*.

An ex-boyfriend texted me out of the blue recently, years after we broke up, to tell me he thought of me often.

"What kind of thoughts?" I asked. I'd vowed to never talk to him again.

"Love that you've cut a path through life doing exactly what you wanna do. It's inspirational," he said. "It takes tremendous courage to throw it all up in the air and hope that it'll work from day to day, week to week, month to month, year to year. You're very courageous for that," he added. "I still noodle away at the guitar every now and then," he continues. "My motto is, *When I sound good enough to be able to stand to hear myself play, then I'll start practising*."

"I know. I'm stubborn that way," I said.

"That is a good stubborn. I think the proper term (look at me, advising the poet of the 'proper' term) is *tenacity* or *grit*."

"That I have. But few pay me for it," I said.

These questions keep coming up—this *how-do-you-do-it?*, this *what-does-it-take?*—when I admit to being a writer. That's my job, I say, and then I do some other jobs to pay for it. It's the kind of job in which you are accountable to yourself alone. You cannot cheat. All this amounts to: I never have time to do nothing. Nothing has nothing to do with me. There is a salvation in that. It is a blessing in a world where so many people do not know what the purpose of their lives is or why they do what they do, why they seek cheap thrills and social media candy that leaves them feeling even emptier.

I'm constantly on the verge of firing myself but the consequences of quitting my writing job are too hard to face. Why do I still write? Truth is, I cannot *not* write. Writing is its own reward. It is the cake; I can have my cake and eat it. Over the last two decades, I learned this work is essential to who I am. And for that long, I've been carving a space for it, hoping to convince people it *is* my work. In a market economy based on monetizing what we share, on manufacturing scarcity, I had discovered an abundance that I needed no one to provide but myself. Anything else on top of that is, well, the cherry on top. Love like that is contagious.

Today, graduate students struggle to make rent, we have English teachers "who have never had pensions" and many teachers and scholars who have taught for decades "have never had a permanent job"; this makes up "a growing group of precarious workers that Canadian universities rely on to educate the next generation."[30]

Is this a lament? Yes, and a praise for doing what you love and surviving it. Despite all this, I'm here, still writing, still fighting, which is perhaps why we can get away with not paying for it. It is the happiness money can't buy.

We say that the arts are worth dying for. Is that why we let people perish on the artist's "salary"? "Arts and culture contributed $54.8 billion to Canada's GDP and 914,000 jobs, representing 4.4 percent of all Canadian workers in 2021."[31] The Canadian book industry is worth almost $2 billion (pre-pandemic). There is no doubt we value writers' work; let's pay us better. Until then, I'll keep getting… that look.

A Sack of Salt

The kitchen was the place to be. It was unlikely you'd be asked what you are doing in the kitchen or why you weren't doing something else. My mother would ask: *Are you hungry?*

If you were not headed for the kitchen, the food smells would lure you in. My mother conducted this symphony of steam, spices and marinades with something akin to making magic potions. Her hands fluttering over the pot with crushed herbs as if she was casting spells. Stories and happenings were sprinkled in for good measure. The ingredient of love palpable.

Any activity in the kitchen was inevitably hemmed in with words: a pot simmers on the stove while a story brews in the mouth. Even shopping for the freshest meats and vegetables from the market was a source of stories to unpack with the groceries. The butcher and the farmers were directly involved with the food they sold and they, too, had stories to tell. The only kind of market was the farmer's market.

Sometimes, my dad made an appearance as a supporting character to orchestrate one of his specialties: the green salad with yogurt dressing topped with sliced radishes, the white and red of the radishes so bright on the green, so translucently thin. He prides himself on how thin. *Kyopolou,* a delicious salsa-like spread with roasted peppers and roasted eggplant, fresh tomato, parsley, garlic and olive oil, was another dish he takes pride in, and so is *tarator* (cold cucumber soup). Not to mention the crunchy pickled vegetable and cabbage alchemy he conducted in the basement. I could never get enough of the crisp delicious juice the cabbage came out of. My dad added a beet to turn it pink. I would drink it as if my life depended on it. When guessing my age, people consistently make me a good ten years younger. I have a secret suspicion it was all that pickle juice. I must have drunk my weight in pink pickled cabbage juice.

The kitchen holds secrets a cookbook might never capture. I usually helped chop, hovered over pots, licked spoons and pans, lingered, washed dishes or just got in the way. The kitchen most of all was a place where we became permeable to wisdom. Part of the meal preparation was all the things that got resolved or worked out in the process. Somehow, it was safer to be doing something while talking about what troubles, upsets or nags at you. On one such occasion, while I lamented about some trouble with a friend, my mother said, "To get to know someone, you have to eat a sack of salt with them." I tried to imagine how big a sack was (fifty kilograms, to be precise) and saw how little salt she put in the *guyvetch* she was composing.

During meals, time expanded into a space of stories and laughter. It felt endless. On a different continent, in Nigeria, we sat around the table for more than one meal a day. Mealtime was not just a delight to the palate but also an open space, like a field, where things inevitably come up. A place where life got sorted out, celebrated, resolved, made up and healed after daily challenges, disagreements or misalignments. It was a consequence of sitting face to face and, like a poem, you could not define it or measure it.

Mealtimes were democratic. Everyone got a chance to tell a version of the story (their version), add details others missed or share an idea, thought or joke. Some jokes and stories became staples. All this over my mom's version of a delicious Nigerian stew (with the vegetables we grew in our garden) or over *banitza* made with homemade feta and hand-stretched crusts. These crusts were troublesome; they would tear if you lost focus or were not in tune with how far dough can stretch. These moments at the table became close studies of point of view, of consequence, where even us kids had an equal voice. We weighed in on what happened away from the heat of the moment, away from the trouble we got in. And we got into plenty of trouble. The time at the table over food allowed us to pull on these issues gently, to stretch them like dough. The dough would tear if you were not patient or careful or in tune with how a conversation works. Time, too, stretched and paused for us and in those moments, we became as pliable as dough and more open to understanding.

The first time I cooked for myself was out of a sense of revolt. I was about ten and fell out with my dad. I was so upset I decided I would cook for myself from that day on. I made *mish-mash* (sautéed onions, roasted peppers, tomatoes, feta, eggs and parsley). It is hard to mess up *mish-mash*. I was going to prove myself and looked around to see what else was available. I added cucumbers. I spent the afternoon making bread. By dinner time, I'd made up with my dad and shared what I cooked. He showed his goodwill by eating my concoctions. Later, we laughed about how the cucumbers resisted the oil and were not great collaborators in stir-fries. I'd never seen anyone fry cucumber; I thought I was being creative. The bread was better suited as the dwarf bread from Terry Pratchett's Discworld series where it is used as a weapon and only eaten as a last resort. That day, I did not cook with love but more out of frustration and hubris, and the outcome was unpalatable. I do not remember ever doing that again.

You do not think something is special, or think of it as a tradition or a ritual, until you begin to miss the good of it. In the United States, while studying for my second master's, I had to learn to cook—out of necessity this time. In Ohio, food was either too sweet or too salty. The complexity of flavour I was used to was as rare in Ohio as an edelweiss flower. I had to come to the rescue of my own tastebuds.

Shopping for the first time was so overwhelming I bought nothing. Not just because I'd never had to navigate a monstrosity of a grocery store like Kroger but also because most things that were supposed to pass for food did not look like food and did not smell like food. I had to take someone's word for it instead. I was buying words on labels and pretty photos. There was no one to whisper the story of the food. Tiny labels on every tomato, apple or pepper not only made little sense but mostly made me sad. What is this place where people have time to label every fruit or vegetable but no time to tell you who grew it? Besides, we bought them by the kilo in Bulgaria. I followed my Thai housemate around. I watched her shop and asked many questions, which she undoubtedly found amusing and probably exhausting. Then, we went home and she fed me one of the delicious dishes she seemed to whip up with such ease. I would call my mother often that first year for the gaps I needed to fill in the recipes. Once I got tired of eating one dish, I took to perfecting another.

I rarely follow the recipes in cookbooks now. After a few decades of home cooking, you get a pretty good sense of what needs to also be there besides what the recipe book suggests.

When I got married, the ritual of home cooking and sitting down for meals was integral in building the dynamics and growing the health of my family. In the United States, I could not fathom how one would eat in front of a TV or microwave a dinner in plastic. We got rid of the TV when the kids were born. I worked hard to preserve non-negotiable dinner time when the four of us sat around the table. It got harder as the kids got older. No one was allowed to schedule anything during dinner time, no electronics at the table, no TV droning on in the background. Regardless of what was going on, once a day, we were all going to sit down and have a meal together. How did my mom make it look so natural and easy?

In a culture of how to best create addictive behaviours and cravings for the cheapest of "food," health appeared to be of little to no priority. I watched how quickly my children's palates narrowed to the taste of hot dogs, mac and cheese, spaghetti and pizza. I had to compete with these limited flavours kids get addicted to. I kept cooking a wider range of dishes and figured out how to hide the vegetables they didn't like. I did not succumb. The effort was worthwhile in the long run, even if the results were disastrous at times. It's so easy to train ourselves out of what is good for our minds and bodies. They remembered again how to be adventurous with flavours. I have been making yogurt for as long as they have been alive. My now grown children still prefer it to the mostly corrupt store-bought variety.

When my sons were in high school, I packed them hot lunches. Some days, I'd offer them money to get pizza or some other cafeteria lunch. "But why? Your food is so much better," my younger son would say. "My friends line up to try it." This secretly delighted me. It gave me the boost to get up early and pack a hot lunch.

Now, my sons tell me to put my cellphone away on the rare occasion I reach for it during dinner. The tradition of sitting together persists. Under the pandemic, both were in pods and bubbles with peers. They sent me photos and notes of things they cooked. Bread, curries, lentil stew, savoury yam pastries, miso soup with no miso in it. Occasionally, I get a call or message from one of them asking what we put in this or that dish. Recently, the two of them were together in San Francisco and decided to make *surmi* (rice, meat, vegetable and spices wrapped in vine leaves). One held the phone and assisted while the other one kneaded the filling. This thrilled me to no end. Food brought us all three together even with borders between us.

My relationship with food has defined not just my relationship with others but also with myself too. Food is a necessity but, more importantly, it binds us and reminds us of who we are. Too much convenience robs us of basic human activities necessary to build connections and relationships. Sitting together for meals secures space and time to remember what children need for healthy development: connection, talking, playing, a healthy home, a community and spaces to make sense of life. Slow food is a celebration, a sustenance, a place to regain a sanity the pace of life cheats us out of. Cooking and eating together weaves memory, stories and connections through ingredients, traditions and cultures and through the simple ritual of eating and time spent together. When we break bread together, we build trust; we nurture and sustain peace.

I saw this most natural of human practices become less common in my own lifetime on a continent that seemed to nourish people with TV dinners in front of a TV. The simple act of sitting down to eat took on the status and stubbornness of a tradition. In a culture of disposable goods (such goods now turned *bads*), a culture of disposable relationships, the dizzying pace prevents us from nurturing such patience. It prevents us from growing our devotion with the simple attention we gift each other.

I wonder how many sacks of salt my kids and I have eaten together. This patience and duration across time, and continuity across cultures and generations, is integral to shaping and sustaining our identities. It's vital to my physical and mental health: a quiet comfort, a happiness that I cannot buy. Cooking secures a space for making something with my hands from scratch the way I make poems. Chopping vegetables takes on the status of a meditation. I will never buy pre-chopped anything. I would not use a food processor. Just me and the vegetables and the knife. I am compelled to share the food I cook with another. Taking pride and responsibility with food is who I am. Extending that to how and where our food comes from is most urgent to nurture the connections across land and species. You are what you eat, but you are also where the food was grown, how you prepare it, what stories you tell about it and with whom you choose to share it. And the circle repeats daily. The empty seat left at the table, my mother tells me, is for the person who could not be there or the guest we do not expect. Word has it, God invited them.

Strung Like Christmas Lights

When spring puts out new leaves, it doesn't think of fall. When I got married, I never thought that in twenty years I'd have to get unmarried; I never imagined the gold seal on our marriage certificate broken. We pledged to grow old together, heads in clouds of white hair, hands linked. My marriage grew old before I did. He moved out in September. We glossed over Thanksgiving. Marked it with a dinner for the four of us. There was no ham or turkey that Christmas. No family, no Christmas.

The kids were three and seven when my husband asked for a separation for the first time. We had just moved to Vancouver to be closer to his job. It took three years of owning our home in the bedroom community of Maple Ridge, and feeling isolated, for us to be ready for the change. It took a couple of long years of being left to deal with his mother, who we helped emigrate from the United States. My husband had not lived with her since he was a teenager and she arrived with issues that began to interfere with our lives, issues I was not willing to hang around for. We finally made the move to Vancouver.

We had just put the kids to bed and were sitting on the indigo-blue couch we had dragged here from Ohio when he popped the question. Life was already full to the brim. I did not want my family pulled apart. I wanted to keep writing. The first of these was impossible without him; the other was threatened, if possible at all. I couldn't imagine having two of everything. The everything we had was already more than plenty. Shuffling kids between homes was good for no one. We could barely keep track of that irreplaceable ducky or monkey in one house. There was no falling asleep without them. It was practical to keep everyone under the same roof, to offset the rising cost of rent and life. We were a good team. After highlighting all the arguments for why we should stay together (mostly me talking), things got quiet. We got busy.

Christmas was his thing: he liked to shop for presents, he loved hanging stockings, he enjoyed hide-wrapping presents and he loved the present rituals on Christmas mornings. Christmas is mostly a blur for me. I avoid shopping in general but even more religiously in December. I have little tolerance for big box stores but at Christmas that tolerance is lower, with the repetitive neurotic music, lights and smells aggressively piped through stores. I have to survive air thickened with anxiety. Each time someone asks me, *Are you ready for Christmas?*, I feel like it is a marathon I am training for, not a holiday to celebrate. And I get asked that question a lot. How do I say I am never ready for Christmas. Was the Virgin Mary ready for Christmas? What would she have said? To make things worse, our anniversary was on December 23, two days before Christmas. The probability of remembering the date, or making it special with all the demands of Christmas, was slim. Each Christmas, I braced myself and weathered through the way one weathers a blizzard. It dampened the mood toward any anniversary celebrations.

I grew up on other continents celebrating New Year's Eve. My family festivities revolved around the time the old year rolled over and we toasted the new one in. It was the time when we said goodbye to the old, put to rest ordeals we had been through, acknowledged accomplishments and successes, and stood on the threshold of the incoming new year filled with new dreams and hope. It is easier for me to get behind that. The presents, the fireworks and sparklers, the staying up past midnight all make more sense on New Year's Eve. It was a communal affair. It felt less lonely. We took stock together of the old year and released our dreams collectively into the next year. I tried that with my husband but he was not too much into the *taking stock* part, or the *dreaming* part.

I have a vivid childhood memory of the new year "back home" in Bulgaria. At the strike of midnight, neighbours would open their doors and weave a *horo*—a line dance—up and down stairs through each other's apartments. In Nigeria, festivities took on different configurations, where adults were in one house and the kids were in a nearby house, usually up to lots of shenanigans, silliness and laughter. Christmas Eve and day were a quiet, subdued ritual where we ate vegetarian dishes like lentil soup, *banitza* and prune compote. The eve of Christmas marked the end of a fast. The rest was some eastern Orthodox hush-hush that was not spoken of too loudly or given much importance. Before the strike of midnight, my parents had figured out how to be home when there was a knock on the door. Us kids ran as fast as we could to open it. We were never fast enough to catch Santa but a big bag of presents sat on the threshold for all of us.

Year after year, the erosion of our relationship continued in slow, imperceptible ways. The light between us dimmed. The shadows my thoughts threw lengthened. Ten years later, he emphatically wanted out. He wanted a separation and then he wanted a divorce. I knew little about such things. I knew people worked stuff out, found ways to co-exist and care for each other, solved their issues and carried on. But his mom was separated and divorced three times. That was a solution familiar to him. And what was familiar to him was alien to me. My parents are still together.

I let him research the details of what it would take to separate a life of twenty years together. I usually did the paperwork in the house. I was the "finance minister." This was paperwork I was not going to do. I did not want it, so that became his thing, like Christmas.

It was at that time that I also discovered, as if unearthing something that had been lying under a rock, that he stayed for those ten years because he feared I might take the kids away. A present that sat wrapped for a long time. All I said was, "I'm not going to give up on the children." This is how communication between us worked or, shall we say, didn't.

The marriage irregularity report was mirrored
and retracted through various reiterations of paperwork.

How the world loses a bit of its meaning each time.
For years before that we fed our   emotion

transportation systems through small house appliances
as if to unscramble what you would not speak of.

I am now used to being your disappointment.

A separation did not just threaten the wholeness of my family; it also threatened my writing. No matter how much you invest in children or writing, neither pays the bills. At the time, he paid the bills. I did not want a broken home and I wanted to keep writing. These were two things I truly cared about. Writing was too important to give up; it was my constant companion. It sustained my passion, and passion is what I needed in my life.

I thought of possible scenarios in which we might be able to stay together. Our sons were thirteen and sixteen this second time around. I was determined to find solutions to keep us together. I am a problem solver, after all. Instead, we stayed reasonable and sane. In the lull of that decade, grief snuck up on me like a fifth season, borne like the lost child between us. Routines kept us conveniently focussed and numbed.

The sentiment *but I don't love you* snaked its way through those years in one form or another, sometimes in subtle ways: when the word *us* meant just three, when *us* meant everyone else except me. Sometimes, the sentiment came in less subtle ways: when I was made to feel like something left in the back of the fridge that had gone bad and had to be cleaned out. When his wedding band came off, it was because he got a rash underneath. Sleeping on the couch was because he snored and neither of us was getting any sleep. I had learned to sleep with earplugs, like a construction worker. I woke up tired.

My dreams, too, began to feel like hard work, perhaps cobbling together another keep-the-family-together plan.

Does this clay pot of ours retain a memory of fire?

I thumb through our poorly recorded etymologies.
I walk backwards in time look for
the threshold on which you loved me.

What are these shards I am putting together worth
when all I end up reclaiming is
the pot's emptiness?

Any attempts at reconciling were met with that terminal *but-I-don't-love-you*. I looked for the man I saw when we met for the first time. How is it possible to live with another for so long and feel so unknown?

There are only so many *but-I-don't-love-yous* you can hear in a lifetime before they begin to take a toll. I got more than my fair share. I didn't think not loving him was an option. He was now the man down the hallway, someone to bump into in the night. I felt more and more a stranger. What did he see that I didn't?

I must have been good at convincing myself the sacrifices were worthwhile. I was apparently also good at making excuses for him: he was reliable, laid back, non-confrontational, we could afford to always have one of us available for the kids, he was a good dad. One of my friends kept pointing to this ability

I have to convince myself it's worthwhile sticking it out. The truth was I wasn't sure what being truly intimate felt like anymore. When she pointed that out more times than I could bear, I began to see that *laid back* really meant not dealing with things that needed dealing with; *non-confrontational* now meant I had to be the bad cop. A nagging suspicion began to eat at me: perhaps it was children he wanted all along, not a wife. A terrible thought to occur twenty years down the road.

My most favourite time of the winter holidays was the time when everyone had opened their presents. It felt like I held my breath through the month of November and most of December. All seemed to grow quiet right after Christmas and my excitement began to build up toward New Year's Eve. The light, too, begins to grow after the winter solstice. That lull between Christmas and New Year's is what I looked forward to. Kids were mostly happy with what they got and expectations were fulfilled, or not.

When my older son was little, he asked Santa for a magic wand. I tried to figure out how I could fulfil his wish. We got him a flute. He was visibly disappointed. I thought making music would be the magic part. No matter how hard we tried, the magic he was after was not something we could buy. The love we have to give is not something we can delegate to a present either. I was missing that other part, the part outside of the present. The part that made the present more than what it was. I was missing what it meant. It turned out a card with words on it was also a lot to ask for and a difficult thing to give.

The last few years we spent "together" you gravitated toward
the stencil of the familiar.   You retreated.   Withdrew.

Slept on the couch for years.

Each time the world became a little less innocent.
I mostly remember   unspoken things.

Who is this "you" that you did not love anymore?

When we finally told the children, they didn't ask any questions. That worried me at first. Of course, we made sure they knew it was not their fault. It appeared not to be as hard on them as it was on me. They seemed used to hearing about separations. From time to time, they'd even utter words of wisdom and comfort: *It's okay, Mom, most of my friends have two houses.* When I told my parents, they exclaimed: *Finally.* As if they knew something I didn't. What is this blind spot that I had not been checking over my shoulder, a spot that I have been continuously running into with so little recognition of what has been right there in the next lane, fixed in the place I cannot see and moving at the same speed as me?

Christmas on this continent has shape-shifted into something of commercial proportions. It is more about appearances: more performance than holiday, more test than celebration. For me, it became something to survive once a year. Magic was never hidden in wrappers. Magic is the thing that happens in the space between us.

The separation and divorce became the next thing I had to survive, just like Christmas. Who gets what? Who stays, who goes, and where? Who gets the kids and for how long? Another adjustment of expectations, surprises and disappointments. What's under that pretty wrapper, under those words, behind that paperwork? I never knew how the hopeful letters I wrote would be answered. A time of holding my breath and repeating, *This too shall pass*, while all along I was trying to take stock of my life and imagine a future without him.

Each time I thought   we hit rock bottom
each time I thought   there couldn't possibly be
anything   more   to lose

the bottom fell out   from under my feet.

There was yet another rock bottom
further down.
Each time I lost   a little more ground
a little more of   what I hold   dear
I become a little more   used to
being disappointed. A little more used
to being   your disappointment.

In the months after the separation, when the whole ordeal hit me hard, the odd unkind word slipped out. Once, my younger son snapped at me: "Stop dissing my dad." That put me right back in the place I wanted to be in the first place. In those moments, I failed to contain the disappointment. I felt like a failure, stalked by the grief that follows. What we aspire to is not always what we actually do. We are that kind of imperfect.

It also occurred to me that my younger son had only known this: our long descent into a separation. I wondered how much his senses had been picking up. When he was a toddler, he would constantly put his arms around both our necks and bring our faces together for a three-way kiss. An eerie thought now, as if he knew all along. This kind of grief follows you like a long tail that keeps the door open and lets gripping winter cold in.

Having a broken heart might sound more metaphor than sensation but heartbreak is physical and palpable. There is a sound to it. It is not the crash of an expensive vase falling off a pedestal. It is more the sound of pulling apart, a hurt in the chest, a tearing. I would wake up to that sound for months before and after the separation. One morning, I tried hating him. Before the day was over, I realized it wasn't my way, even if I had it in me to be mad to the point of hate. I had much to do and it needed my love, not my resentment or anger. I had to pack school lunches, do the laundry, cook dinner, look for jobs, prepare to teach class, steal time to write. There weren't enough hours in the day to be mad, angry or depressed. Besides, feeding that side of me would change me, hurt me more. The to-do list grows much longer when you become a single parent. So, I gave up anger in lieu of checking off the next thing on my list. I gave up resentment in lieu of sleep. I gave up the downward spirals for climbing the unsurmountable mountain of being the one who had to do most things now on her own. Those were my little triumphs in the dark days.

For years I beamed hope like a satellite as if
it will air on all TV stations around the world.

I entertained grief in my house
but I refused to be grief's servant.

I kept stomping out shadows with the verve of someone stomping out a fire threatening to swallow them. Writing kept me sane and patient; doing things for others got me out of the whirlpool in my head that could instantly drag me in its undertow. The closer I got to the light, the smaller the shadows got. I had some good teachers. Shock. Despair. Longing. Missing. Recognition. Epiphany. But my best teacher turned out to be Exhaustion.

This morning a single leaf from last year still clings
to its winter tree shivers in the spring breeze.

I gain a little strength from it and keep going.

❦

After he moved out, my body reverted to a calm I'd forgotten. How to describe this peaceful feeling adequately? A bit like the peaceful feeling I got once Christmas was over. You recognize this kind of missing only when you feel the peace come back. How easy it is to get used to our predicaments to the point where we cannot imagine other possibilities.

A couple of months after Christmas, I thanked him for leaving me. A belated Christmas present of sorts. A birthday present. I thought he might like to hear that, perhaps put some guilt to rest. We managed to keep things amicable between us. I was grateful for that too.

❦

What tipped the scales in the end was the realization that what was worse than a divorce was the kids living with parents in a quietly unhealthy relationship. It might compromise the relationships they forge, how they, too, might settle into what feels familiar like home. I am still left wondering: *Was our relationship as bad as he paints it? Was I too happy-go-lucky, all along prioritizing the positive?*

❦

New living arrangements took shape in the aftermath. Our sons went back and forth between two homes. Our language was altering, and that was altering us. I became even more sensitive to our words: *your house, my house, dad's house, mom's house*. They grated on my ear. It's not just about memory but also our relationship to words. How they nourish or empty us, how they burn or rub the wrong way. How parents set us up for such cycles. That thought terrified me. I don't want my children to bear such burdens.

In hindsight, the distress of hearing *but-I-don't-love-you* was eclipsed by the thought that I couldn't remember a time when he said he did love me.

No one wanted to talk about the next Christmas. And when we did, no one volunteered to put up the tree. I tried to talk myself into it for the sake of the kids but miserably failed in that motivational speech. Christmas, like a marriage, is a communal endeavour. One person does not a Christmas make. I did put up the Christmas lights, though. Their small spark in the holiday night reminded me of each of us: how we appear separate but we are strung to each other through the invisible strings between us. If one of the lights is pulled out, it affects the rest of the lights in the string. We are responsible to keep the connections working.

Grief is a poor landlord.   *A house broken*
woman in disrepair   *riddled with insight.*

Why did it take me so long to let go? I danced with grief. Held it and even loved it. Felt everything it had to give me. But I did not let it move permanently into my house. I had to keep reminding myself to let it go. Let it go through me and then let it slink out the back door. Like a pet you have for a while and then is gone. It leaves you after living its life. I did not know how to do all that. I did not believe I could do it at the time. I had to trust, stop pushing it aside. It comes from a tender place. It comes from true love. It whispers little epiphanies. It mobilized me, left me wiser and stronger somehow. I am more afraid of regret now than grief.

How do I begin all over again? The dread of dating came back to plague me. How do I stand on the edge of this cliff where the ground had fallen out from right underneath my feet? How do I avoid the fear of relationship heights? I dreaded dating to begin with. I also didn't like coming home to an empty house at night. These two competing forces had to battle it out. I wanted to share my life with another. I grew up with the idea that a shared sorrow is half the sorrow, a shared joy is twice the joy. It's how I understand connection and the spaces between two. It is how I want my holidays.

I no longer want to enter this emptiness we created.

I soak up last night's full moon and today's rain as if
they are a prescription   the doctor wrote.

He moved out in the fall. That winter, all I could think of was spring. It was a very long winter. I watched Christmas trees planted inside lit-up houses, furniture moved around to accommodate the brightest of decorations and the biggest of presents. I walked the cold streets of January, stepped over perfectly parched trees abandoned on sidewalks. Their branches shed needles we kicked around on the pavement as if sorrows, as if brittle revelations, as if sharp regrets someone will have to pick up the next day.

When spring unfurls young leaves or pushes out new buds, it doesn't think of the time it will have to let them go. I get up in the morning and look at the expanse of day spread before me. It is up to me. I have so much more energy to devote to dreams and worthwhile things. Somewhere, there is still a blind piece of paper with its gold seal still intact. I was worried I might never again be able to think like spring. But spring did come and even though our marriage grew old before we did, I for one felt much, much younger. Even my laughter, which I missed for a while, startled me, seemed alien, but perhaps that is what it always sounds like to someone hearing it for the first time.

Bringing the Roots Home

After three years of travelling and living on and off the land, looking for community, giving up technology to track the effect it has on his mind, my son is going to university this fall. It's the kind of school he has been looking for, where he can pose important questions and design his course of study. It's a relatively small school, where it might be possible to know almost everyone. He decided this would be a less lonely way to find like-minded people. It's the most expensive university in the area but he is determined so he found a job to earn his portion of tuition. This summer, he has been teaching bushcraft and wilderness survival skills, doing renovation work and yard landscaping. He has been digging things up.

One day, after clearing an unwanted patch of Solomon's seal in a client's yard, he brought a bag of roots home. The roots, he told me, have a variety of medicinal properties. He wanted to try different things: slice them, roast them, dry them, make decoctions and tinctures. All his life, he has wanted to bring the outdoors in, to do things that we are not equipped for. Sometimes, I could provide him with the space or tools he needed but more often, I couldn't. That's where the rub is. I know that what he's doing is important but I'm weary of the house filled with plants, animals and the wild. When he was a child, it was easier to appease him with books on edible and medicinal plants or wilderness survival. Then, he did not want to read about the outdoors; he wanted to *be* the outdoors.

Right now, there are roots drying on newspapers on the patio, roots on my front porch and roots in various states of de-rooting in the fridge. Yesterday, he sliced some and wanted to dry them.

"Sure, use our south-facing patio. Summer's perfect for drying things," I said.

"It has to be a dark place otherwise they lose medicinal properties," he countered.

I had trouble with the roots coming into the house to begin with and now we had to rethink closet space. I get upset at how much he assumes our house can be turned into a centre for gathering, sorting, storing and making things. Leather sandal soles treated with linseed oil have been drying on the patio for weeks.

It was a long three years when he decided to go to England and travel through Europe without having a cellphone, computer or tablet. The only thing I received as news was handwritten letters. He even made the ink he used. The ink was made from oak galls (they look like pimples that form around a bug, maybe a wasp, that perhaps tried to burrow in). He boiled them in a tin can over a fire. The colour comes from the tannins. The ink in medieval manuscripts was usually made from these but often with iron added to turn it black. When I saw the envelope with the reddish-brown ink slip through the mail slot in my door, time stopped. I read every word like it was life giving, like it was breath. Of course, it would have taken a good ten days for the letter to arrive so this was a snapshot of a past moment, the way light travels from a star: you know that what you see is not the star right now. What you perceive right now is a kind of history. While I was reading one of those letters, I was eating blueberries.

One fell, rolled down the page, obliterating a string of letters with the splash of drops. It terrified me that I could miss a syllable, misread a word. I discovered the ink was water-soluble and that put the letters at further risk in their arrival.

I am a writer and my biggest clutter is books and piles of paper. I keep trying to clear the house of stuff. It is akin to clearing the mind before sitting down to write. In the material world we live in, things pile up. Anything the kids don't want in their rooms ends up on the landing. I'm aware that my house is a centre for empowering ourselves with what we can accomplish if we set our minds to it. It is a centre for resistance for each of us, a pushback against the warped and consumer world we live in. We refuse to feel powerless to do things for ourselves in a world that constantly says you'd better leave it to the experts. But that does not help me deal with the breadth and range of compromise and accommodation I have to make within the small spaces of our urban home.

My needs are simple. A laptop, a table and a seat. Preferably a seat close to the ground and close to a window. I use a big pillow to sit on and my breakfast-in-bed table for writing. Years ago, my husband gave me this table as a gift even though I was never much of a breakfast person. After twenty years of marriage and parenting, we parted ways. The odds of getting breakfast in bed now are even smaller. We grew roots together for so long, then had to unearth, uproot and move them, to cultivate them somewhere else. There's no guarantee they'll take. We were a good team raising our children but after the kids were grown, there wasn't much left between us. We shared some memories, many of which were remembered so differently, they might as well have been different memories. Different lives, even. Had we changed? Or maybe the problem was that we hadn't changed?

Or maybe just one of us had? Ultimately, we got tired of trying. I'm still wondering how it's possible to un-love someone after so long.

My older son has always been determined, and consistently so, to do what he's passionate about. I cannot blame him. Perhaps I gave him too good of an example. But I don't need much to pursue my passion and he needs the whole of the outdoors and preferably away from the city. He is a bare-feet-on-the-ground kind of kid. He is a can-we-eat-this-plant and can-we-hunt-that-squirrel kind of kid. Not a kid anymore. He can build a shelter and he can make a bow drill fire. He would gather the materials himself; no ready-made kits from Amazon.

This is not a phase. He has always brought things home. I do that, too, but I stick to shells, rocks and twigs. My parents drew the line at an arm-length log I dragged down from a mountain. They made me leave it on the landing outside the door of our apartment on the eighth floor. It turned into a conversation piece for anyone who came to our door. My son brings home skins, bark, antlers, bones and teeth.

We're in the midst of de-mothing his room. He found the culprits in buffalo wool he brought from Ontario, all the way from the other side of the country. Wool so delicious no moth could resist it. His nature drawer had turned into a moth incubator. Most of his closet is now in plastic bags and for weeks, he's been sunning and freezing things that could be potential moth territory.

In the midst of all this, he brings home this huge bag of Solomon's seal roots. Unwanted roots he cleaned out of someone's yard. They look like hairy ginger roots. At 10:00 p.m., the sink is full of roots. It's time to slice and dry. At 10:00 p.m., I'm telling my mind and body to slow down and prepare to sleep.

Time is short. To be a writer means you have to figure out how to stretch time like pizza dough. I have to play nice with time, pull gently on the thinning crust. Split the seconds to get more out of them amidst all I have to do. And I still do not get enough. It's a constant balancing act. I strive to clear out of my way what has to get done, to free time and space for what I love to do. My son is doing the same. But every time I feel I've put something to rest, like the kitchen or laundry or vacuuming, and sit to do my work in my little corner, at my little breakfast-in-bed-turned-computer-table, on an air cushion that keeps me balancing even when I sit, I find out that there's something else that's urgently going on.

I seek solitude. This is how I resist. I seek quiet spaces where I make sense of the world and of myself, where I recognize when I'm being unfair, when I've been pushed too far or have pushed someone too far. "Solitude is a silent storm that breaks down all our dead branches; yet it sends our living roots deeper into the living heart of the living earth," writes Kahlil Gibran.[32] Solitude is my rebellion against the world of multiple screens, social media predictability and distraction, decibels haunting urban streets. It is not only our time that gets fragmented and cannibalized but along with it our attention, compassion, understanding and imagination. In an interview at the 2024 Vancouver Writers Fest discussing his book *On Freedom,* Timothy Snyder said, "If we don't know who we are, we cannot be free."[33] Nothing is lost once I secure solitude. Once there, I reach for something less fleeting, something I can hold on to, something I can grow, like a root. Time expands and I feel a luxury the rushing world cannot offer. Solitude anchors me.

My son does the same. It's just that he literally brings the roots home, the woven baskets, the arrows, the hides. The other day, it was the thin branches of a tree that he said were perfect material for making arrows. This week, he's using them to teach kids at the outdoor camp. He's full of stories and music. He's full of fire. This delights me—but also makes me feel inadequate as a parent. On some days, I feel I fail him.

We both resist the divisive nature of our world today, the economic schizophrenia and political psychosis. To make this possible and positive, I have to love harder than I've ever done before. Love not as something that comes naturally, but love practiced consciously, as resistance, to counter the confusion, anger and hate I encounter daily. I was happy to discover that Snyder also thinks love is essential to freedom. He also said: "Freedom has to mean loving things and it has to mean admitting that you love things. And that is why it always requires a little bit of courage."[34]

We live in the city. We can't bring the whole of the outdoors inside our living space. The city places too many constraints on roots. Covers and strangles them with concrete. Smooths out the stumps with a stump grinder so even the memory of a tree is obliterated. Or eradicates them altogether and truncates our memory. He doesn't like the city. I get upset when he pushes too far, which overshadows the roots that bind us.

We're both makers. He makes things with his hands, I dig up the roots of words, write poems. He does literally what I tend to metaphorically. Both are political acts of empowerment, resistance and resilience. Both are ways of claiming our freedom, our memory, our connection to land. Both of us pursue our passions and make sense of the senseless world we have to live in these days. We need poems, like bread, but we also need bread to eat so we can write poems. He makes us bread with a sourdough starter he has been nursing on top of the fridge. I make yogurt.

In our love for roots and trees, we sit with them, let them nurture and heal us. He sketches them. Our imaginations follow their dendritic thoughts. We resist the simplification of our complex ecologies. "When we have learned how to listen to trees," poet Hermann Hesse writes, "then the brevity and the quickness and the childlike hastiness of our thoughts achieve an incomparable joy."[35] We listen to these ancient beings. These roots and branches and leaves are the ways the earth thinks. We have a need to be part of this conversation. I find joy in these small spaces and interactions. It's also where my hope lives in an age of digital atrophies and addictions.

Both my son and I work on roots in different ways in a culture that is bent on eradicating them, cutting and binding them, or in simply being oblivious to them. We are only now beginning to discover the many ways trees talk to each other through their roots. Botanist Diana Beresford-Kroeger will tell you that trees and forests also talk to us through a low frequency that affects our chemistry and nervous systems.[36] Experts are now telling us what we have known for a long time. Culture binds us to our roots. Roots talk to us. In this conversation with what is other than human, we become more human. When our human roots connect to their larger and wiser ways, we become more porous, more fluid, more whole. When our roots speak to the roots of other people, we build powerful mycelial networks. When our roots speak to the ki in the world, we connect to the wilderness within us. To complete the Snyder quote I began earlier: "We don't know who we are unless we have other people in our lives and if we don't know who we are, we cannot be free."[37] The future looks brighter that way.

After two years at Quest University, my son's university left him. The pandemic forced both my kids to go online. Now that less screen time was not an option, my son used the research he had done to create a resource for schoolteachers and parents that might help them with managing kids and screens. He wrote the book, made the art for it, designed the book and cover, did the editing and published it. His book, *Screenfarers: Nurturing Deliberate Action in a Digital World,* was the result of that pursuit.[38] He knows what he needs to do and does it. How can I not be proud. Neither of my kids went back to finish their degrees after the pandemic disrupted their studies. There is talk this year he might, after all, go back to finish what he started.

After decades of living away from home, I went to visit my parents. I didn't see my log on the landing outside their front door and assumed they'd finally thrown it out. Instead, I found it inside, in the living room, displayed in the most prominent place above the TV.

Later, I planted some of those Solomon's seal roots my son brought home in a pot on my patio. They have faithfully been coming up every year to remind me of how we persist, how we do not give up, with their white blooms strung like tears, like dew, even when he is away and pursuing his passions elsewhere.

He Loves Me, *He* Loves Me Not

In the Murky Waters of Online Dating

There was no way I was going to get on a dating site. It was a desperate move. I had absorbed this attitude, somehow, and was committed to it. Who looks for a partner online? It turns out about one-third of married couples between 2005 and 2012 met online (according to Aziz Ansari in his book *Modern Romance*[39]). This was a number bigger than meeting through friends and school combined. What was wrong with me then? After my significant other became an insignificant other, after my divorce, I was faced with the daunting task of how to begin this relationship thing all over again.

A friend asked me about the man of my dreams. If a chicken drumstick in my dreams is the size of spaghetti squash, did I really want to meet the man of my dreams? We think we know what we want but the guy I imagined wasn't anything like the man I married. Why would it be different this time? Our brains are complex: we have three layers to them. To make it even more complicated, our rational brain is the thinnest layer, as if it was an afterthought of evolution. It has its own agenda to push while the limbic and reptilian brains cannot be rationalized. "The jurisdiction of will is limited to the latest brain," or the rational brain, while "emotional life can be influenced but not commanded." [40] The reptilian brain has no emotional life.

(At least, so says the book *A General Theory of Love*.) *Good luck*, says Evolution. These different brains are passive-aggressively manipulating each other. Or screaming at each other. Am I the referee? No wonder I am so exhausted.

I didn't want to date anyone from my writing community. In the mid-forties range, the pool was a bit thin. For some, it's a lifestyle choice, which is probably a nicer way of saying no one will put up with them. I didn't want to date anyone from work, yoga or where I live. If things don't go well, I will keep running into them. I wasn't doing much to meet people outside of these groups. My life is streamlined, almost aerodynamic. I don't hang out in pubs. With the five to ten flashing screens, the noise and the drinking, I would more likely become an alcoholic than meet a man I like.

The grocery store? Glance up, scan for potential guy between the meat and the milk aisles? I can make it one-stop shopping but I had no idea what aisles the handsome and sane guys hung out in. The painfully young staff is no help either. This was more than not fun; it was unpalatable, utterly inelegant. Besides, once I go into a store, there's only one thought on my mind: *How quickly can I get out?*

A friend told me of the guys she was meeting online. Most sounded like decent men. Another friend married a woman he met on OkCupid. I began to doubt my preconceived notion. Is it okay, Cupid? Coming home to an empty house was not how I wanted to spend the rest of my life. And the short dark days of winter were closing in.

On one of these December nights, between the encouragements from friends and coming home to no one, I succumbed. I stopped putting up a fight and put up a profile instead. I took a peek at Plenty of Fish (PoF). I saw a couple of profiles and faces

I liked. Before I knew it, I had written something that passed for a profile. I have never fished in my life. Now, I was going to fish metaphorically. I was inundated with messages, none of which were from the guys that caught my eye. I feared I wouldn't last twenty-four hours. I was being browsed through. Men were mouthing the words on my profile and ogling my photos—though it felt more like *oooogling*. Sometimes, my imagination isn't my friend. I hid my profile that night. I couldn't bear the thought of guys staring at me while I slept.

Guys-ville (as I began to call it) is a strange place to navigate. There was the guy-who-likes-bullet-points, the sports aficionado (usually posed with bikes or sports gear). With one of them, I learned it is useless to engage in intellectual swashbuckling on PoF. Then, there was the man-who-compares-women-to-fruit (in this case, mango), and Wolf-man, who had an answer for everything while looking deep into my eyes, but we got hung up a bit on who is responsible for contraception. Then, there was Burger-face, likely posed by a grill or a four-by-four. There was heavily-tattooed-dude and biceps-dude, the guy-much-older-than-his-photo and the man-who-rejects-you-first. None of these were my type. Not to mention the guy-who-tempts-you-with-money-and-property: fuzzy picture of his face with shades, but nice roof and deck. There was the guy-who-will-be-happy-with-you-in-your-sweat-pants but he bored me talking about minutia. I did not spend much time on the younger-guy-looking-for-older-women or the one who sent me a link to a Victoria's Secret's teddy. Then, there was the guy-who-wants-to-be-my-bosom-buddy and commiserate with me on his lack of success on dating sites. The guy-married-to-his-darkness has been there for so long he's used to not getting what he wants. Trying to lighten life a little in the conversations was like, as he put it, "giving a glass of milk to someone who is lactose intolerant." And of course, there was polyamorous-dude, who wrote lovely volumes of texts and brought down the stars for me; too bad it was in the poly edition.

The ones that I had a soft spot for were most-memorable-guy, who said no one is perfect. He was looking for a woman who was the right kind of imperfect for him. Poetically, that appealed to me. But he was not the one either. There was invisible-man, surprisingly quite a few, who, for one reason or another, were not willing to show their faces. One of these invisible men broke my heart. And there was the guy-with-the-irreverent-hilarious-profile, who makes you think he is either crazy or brilliant.

When I shared with friends I was on a dating site, I noticed the reserved look in their eyes, the condemnation in the crimped corner of the mouth, the quick change of topic, the silence at the end of the phone. My parents thought it was dangerous. I gave myself a week.

The variables that had to align seemed impossibly numerous. Looks, voice, smell, touch, taste. And we have more than these five Aristotelian senses. What about intuition, which constantly whispers under the radar of my rational mind? None of these helped me online. We'd not even ventured into age differences, how long we last in relationships, the presence or absence of children, habits, pet peeves or deal breakers, all further complicated by the lives we'd lived. We likely had preferences regarding age, religion, pets and, lately, it looks like we should add politics. Sense of humour was close to the top of my list. Then, there are our needs, wants and fantasies. "No algorithm can predict in advance whether two people will make a good couple. The task is virtually impossible. Humans are not products," writes Ansari.[41] In other words, it is easier to give up. Out of these numerous considerations, the most important ones cannot be put in a profile. On the dating site, we're all a bunch of words open to interpretation. Dating online is a misnomer. The dating had not even started.

Anthropologist Helen Fisher, I believe, will tell you that your brain is your best algorithm. No dating service can do what the human brain can do. She would know; she helps the dating services with their algorithms. Most of us sound so good online. The moment you lay eyes on each other, however, that knowing is instantaneous, like a lighting flash. Then, you count, and wait, for the thunder to measure the distance between you.

The whole dating online experience felt demanding, time consuming and damning. Responding to messages, arranging dates, zeroing in on times to meet, deciding if there are any prospects—it was a full-time job, both emotionally and physically. Aligning the variables I wanted in a partner was further complicated by the fact that I don't always know what I am looking for until I see it. (It was much harder than finding that place to rent where sidewalks took a top-of-the-list place.) Was I choosing based on what I didn't want? A kind of elimination process? Words are abstractions. Some men fantasize about strong confident women, are attracted to them, but when they get one, they don't know what to do with her. Do we want more than we can handle?

Initially, I met one of the invisible men. He was afraid to put up photos on his profile so he sent them to me privately. We dated for a number of months. In hindsight, too many. We had a couple of blissful weeks over Christmas and New Year's, when the breakups began. He left me a dozen times, came back about the same number of times, minus one. I stuck with him for seven months through his turmoils and doubts and in the end regretted it. Even though he had moved out, he had not resolved the complications of his marriage; I had no doubt my separation and divorce papers would eventually be signed. He kept me a secret. It took me a while to figure out he had an alcohol problem; he held his liquor too well. He had fantasies I didn't want to share. I learned what being a rebound means.

Worst of all, he had a bad case of *jealous*. I caught him looking at my day planner and messages on my phone. The lack of trust was maddening. I realized that in those interludes in which he left me, he spent time with other women. Then, he came crawling back to me, singing my praises and full of regret. I was puzzled he would tell me about it. I could not wrap my head around why he did that. Perhaps that way he did not think he was cheating on me? I guess if you're a cheater, you're going to think everyone else is a cheater, which explained the debilitating jealousy. He had no reason to be jealous. Each of these things crept up on me slowly, red flags I shouldn't have ignored.

Friends told me I was making too many excuses for him. They were right but I couldn't hear them at the time. I thought

I'd be strong enough but eventually it wore me down. I secretly hoped the sacrifice I was making would pay off in the end. *No pain, no gain* was the damning motto running through my head. Eventually, I had to let him go despite the dissonances and disagreements between the various layers of my brain. *No pain, no pain,* counters my yoga teacher. He was back on PoF that week and would chat me up when business was slow. His profile still sounded appealing but now I knew what stood behind the words.

We put ourselves into words, like a jacket one wears, but the lining is what will be next to your skin. Three years later, he contacted me and said he was a new man and did not drink anymore. At that point, it seemed commitment was his problem. I did not wait around to find out. *No pain, no pain* is what I am after now. Sadly, I think he was more fun when he was drunk.

The human drive to love is unquenchable. Intimacy, love, eros had become my new passion. Aspects of romantic love span the reptilian, limbic and neocortical brains. Love, like poetry, is a kind of integrating force that makes the heart leap and the soul glad. "The psychic grammar of love is mysterious," writes Lisa Appignanesi in *All About Love*.[42] Love cannot be reduced to a rational transaction. Is love the mycelial network that holds our spiritual ecology together? There was nothing wrong with me when I felt pulled in different directions. It's normal to feel conflicted and divided. I knew better when I found myself torn between being attracted to someone while also knowing they were *not* good for me.

Why are we embarrassed to admit we are seeking a romantic partner? Sure, some people give online dating a bad name.

You will find everything there from the profound to the profane. Judgement lies dormant even with friends and family. I felt the embarrassment, the shame, but I didn't want to succumb to it nor feed it. Statistics were on my side. I think of the invisible men (and women) on the site who fear to show their faces. Why is it more acceptable to be depressed and lonely than to admit we are social creatures who need intimacy to thrive? That is the real shame.

There came a point when I knew too much about many of the faces circulating on the site's banner. They began to feel like family. I was on and off for about nine months. Long enough for this baby of an adventure to come to term. Long enough for some men to forget they had talked to me. Long enough that men who never bothered to respond eventually contacted me. I was about to delete my profile and be done with that episode of my life when I spotted *him*. He had just joined PoF after agonizing over online dating for a while, too, and was not sure this was how he wanted to meet a woman. The curious thing was that you would not have learned much about him from his profile. My first thought after reading it was, *This man is either crazy or hilarious*.

"Too funny to be true," I wrote.

He responded with, "Will let you in on a secret. Only half of my profile is true. The other half, well, it's not true either."

I found out he was not a *bipolar, binge-drinking, cannibal dwarf who can only hold a job down for two weeks* (as he'd written in his profile) but a kind man who is adventurous and not reckless. His profile interests—*wrestling alligators, motivational speaker for porn stars and playing checkers with the tooth fairy*—were replaced with collector of music, interviewing artists, and writing album reviews. The wrestling with alligators seems nothing compared to the social work he does in the single room occupancy hotels of Vancouver, which house people with substance use disorders and mental illness. It takes something special to be able to do this work, and for decades. We moved from the crowded stagnant fishpond to the beach with the rolling surf and laughter.

We are in our tenth year now. It has been sweet. I didn't think there could be anything better than tiramisu but that first year was better. Once, I saw tiramisu advertised as *the most fun you can have in public*; another time, it was called *sex in a pan*. But there is the work too. Lisa Appignanesi reminds us: "Love needs tending. It also seems to need a spirit of generosity and emotional intelligence in which the lines of privacy and togetherness can be redrawn."[43] I am sure psychologist John Gottman would concur: generosity and kindness are what ultimately keep couples together. And my man has such potential for the generosity and kindness it takes. Finding someone is just the beginning.

No relationship is perfect. We have our quirks and quarks. We have our snags and some of them are enough to drive me crazy, but we talk through it. We go through ups and downs; this is no happily-ever-after fairy tale. What has kept us together through thick and thin—we have had some really hard moments—is being kind, keeping an open heart, and instead of being mean, we practice what we mean, practice generosity towards each other. And clearing doubts: there is no doubt we are committed to each other. Ten years in, I can say he has a good and kind heart. Most of all, we are both willing to learn and grow together in that learning. How normal that feels. We laugh things off. How sane that is. And all that time spent looking for this special someone is redeemed by the way he still looks at me.

Market Arguments Do Not Work

for Those Who Cannot Take Part in the Market

It's an accomplishment these days to live in one place for a long time; to age in place is near impossible. I have lived for twenty years now in my co-operative housing complex in the False Creek South neighbourhood. My next-door neighbour has lived here for forty years. We are one of five co-ops built on city-owned land between Cambie and Granville bridges, right across from the concrete jungle and wind tunnels of downtown Vancouver. Amidst a park and urban forest, which attract countless tourists and visitors, we grow a tight-knit community in connected and dignified spaces.

Neither rental nor social housing, our co-op has the responsibilities of a homeowner but we trade financial equity for social capital. Members own the buildings and run the co-op; we rent the land from the city. The mixed-income model allows for internal subsidies for those of us who find themselves in volatile family circumstances, insecure jobs or fixed incomes. When I became a single parent, I paid half of my housing charge for a year. No one knows how much you make when you walk out your door.

On October 21, 2021, residents were shocked to discover that in phase two of a recent redevelopment plan for False Creek South, a plan hatched behind closed doors by the real estate department at city hall, our co-op buildings were erased from the map. The community only had a few days to digest the news before it went to council for a vote. There are many ways to lose your home; fires, floods and earthquakes change lives overnight. Then, there's The Market. Our sixty-year land lease has protected us from The Market so far. The greedy glass eye of developers, and the city, are burning holes of worry in our neighbourhood.

In his article, "Canada's Dual Housing Policy: Assisting Owners, Neglecting Renters," J. David Hulchanski diagnoses: "Only 5 percent of Canada's households live in non-market social housing… the smallest social housing sector of any western nation except the United States."[44] In British Columbia, there are 270 housing co-ops, 112 of which are in Vancouver and 57 of those are on city land.

The problematic redevelopment plan was preceded this summer with an untested lease-renewal framework for the fifty-seven co-ops whose leases expire in the next twenty years. The leases of two of the co-ops here are now expired; ours expires in 2036. The public consultation process was fraught with inaccurate information. The city keeps classifying co-ops under subsidized housing but we do not get handouts from the city. Subsidized luxury condos, which do, don't get listed as subsidized housing. It keeps promoting the myth that more market housing is needed to pay for non-market housing. If that was true, we would have a lot more affordable homes right now. The proposed lease framework was not modelled on co-op data to secure the survival of the delicate balancing act of the organism that is a co-op. It attempted to tie our housing charges to the market. Over sixty of us lined up to speak on July 7, 2021, when it had to be voted in. I sent an open letter to council and the *The Georgia Straight*[45] and my own reciprocal survey[46] to city hall in response to their poor survey claiming to engage with citizens from Vancouver. That day, city staff and council got a crash-course on co-ops but we did not feel we got transparency or bargaining in good faith. We secured an amendment that tied housing charges to average renters' income instead of average Vancouver income; not ideal, but at least co-ops avoided the death sentence that day. No leases have been signed to date.

Not only was there no financial reporting to justify this new plan to the public but it also lacked any environmental or social impact assessments. Experts were scratching their heads. It proposed to move our co-ops to a row of six-storey buildings along busy Sixth Avenue. To accomplish this, they will have to destroy a rare urban forest that not only protects the buildings from the river of traffic but has also become a walking highway for many since the pandemic. Our homes will become pollution and noise barriers for future luxury condos. Our building—replaced with grass and some saplings. Affordable housing will be reduced significantly on the Creek in favour of market rentals (from the current 56 percent to 34 percent, half of which will be people already living here). Just for the 5 co-ops on False Creek, that means displacing 517 households, predominantly families, 1,180 members, 50 percent of whom make under $60,000 and 17 percent of whom make under $30,000 a year.

Destroying well-maintained buildings should not just be unthinkable but also legally questionable in a crisis where market rentals are no longer affordable to low- and middle-income earners like me. Regular no-fault evictions are now a social and health hazard. The growing gap between income and housing cost is pushing middle-income earners into the margins. We get the message: we do not deserve to live in quiet and beautiful places. The plan displays the ethical and moral poverty we have come to understand as The Market.

Co-operatives emerged in the 1800s as an alternative to protect people from the market. Of course, they are inconvenient; it's in their DNA to serve people, not finance. They provide stability to neighbourhoods and security of tenure. Community oriented and invested with social capital, our housing co-op is a hub of education, connection and belonging. Many original members are still here.

In the 1970s, False Creek was polluted industrial land that was not only an eye sore but also threatened property values in the area. The government sealed the land and built a density that was unheard of at the time; some claimed it would turn into a slum.[47] But this ground-oriented neighbourhood became world renowned for its visionary forward-thinking urban plan. *Plan* is the operative word here. A community so successful in integrating and maintaining a mix of lower-, middle- and higher-income residents that it deserves heritage status. I am not sure if Vancouver has seen this kind of urban planning since.

In the spirit of growing what has proven so successful, our community has been negotiating with the city for over fifteen years toward adding density to the area aligned with its founding principles. We have a neighbourhood plan (RePlan), which includes much needed senior housing to free up family units for new families, a kind of intergenerational hub, a campus of care. In 2018, council approved the adoption of the "False Creek South Provisional Vision Statement and Guiding Planning Principles"[48] but it was put on hold to focus on lease renewals. Now we have a less-than-ideal lease-renewal framework and a problematic redevelopment plan that overrode the community vision and plan.

Little Mountain is a tragic example of what happens when the BC Conservative government (that paraded as BC Liberals) messes with very affordable housing. People were evicted from their homes, 238 units were bulldozed, the community scattered. Developer Holborn got hundreds of millions of dollars in free loans for eighteen years, with no deadline for the replacement of the homes. That's what I call subsidized destruction of housing. This is how the city subsidizes developers instead of its own citizens. Currently, Holborn is in the news again for neglect of the Dunsmuir Hotel, built in 1907. In 2013, they evicted 167 low-income tenants and have not only kept this heritage building empty for the last decade but also neglected it so badly it was declared a danger to the public and was voted by council to be demolished within twenty-one days. Why is such neglect not a crime?

There's no way to take Little Mountain back. If you walk by the site today, there is a sign on the fence enclosing the area that says, "Great stories take time to tell." The irony. There is no housing yet, let alone affordable housing. Recently, council voted to exempt Holborn's social housing requirements at Little Mountain for the first two phases of the project's redevelopment. And so, on and on it goes. By my calculations, Holborn owes Vancouver citizens 405 affordable units before they build any market anything. This is a story that will take long to tell because Holborn does not seem to be in it for providing homes at all.

Determined not to become the next Little Mountain, or the next Olympic Village fiasco—which promised citizens two-thirds affordable housing and instead spent unjustified amounts of public money to eventually deliver poorly built and predominantly market condos[49]—we rolled up our communal sleeves.

If you want affordable housing for families and essential and frontline workers, you should protect housing that already exists and provide land at reasonable cost for future additions. We should consider such housing an essential service. What Marc

Lee said in 2021 is still valid today: "Non-market housing on public/community-owned land is the key to achieving the public goal of affordable housing over the long-term."[50] Governments around the world are waking up to this fact. Our city hall only seems to wake up from the developer's kiss. Their primitive and blunt market tools do not serve communities; they have no way to compute or comprehend social capital built into neighbourhoods. Little has been done to dampen escalating land cost. Do they really not understand how co-ops work? Is that ignorance? Arrogance? Malice? "Ignorance, allied with power, is the most ferocious enemy justice can have," writes James Baldwin.[51] Arrogance and malice are worse.

Not only were our perfectly good buildings on the chopping block but sixty-year-old trees in an urban forest also have to be destroyed to accommodate this real estate plan on public land. Trees are not "expensive ornaments" but essential for mental, physical and community health, argues Amy Fleming in "The Importance of Urban Forests."[52] The New York City park department calculated how much money the city was saving putting the trees to work. They calculated that "the benefits added up to $120m a year. (Compare that to the $22m annual parks department expenditure.) There were $28m worth of energy savings, $5m worth of air quality improvements and $36m of costs avoided in mitigating storm water flooding."[53] From grass-root movements to the United Nation's 2016 Habitat III conference, people are organizing to protect urban trees. As I am working on this piece, the hearing on abolishing the 133-year-old parks board and altering the charter is going on at city hall with little to no public consultation. I am number 98 on the speakers list. This, with the background of atmospheric rivers, heat domes and floods that recently claimed lives.

Every morning, I wake up to the shadows the downtown towers throw. How many sit empty? How many are remotely adequate for families? Friends who live in these high-rises don't know their neighbours. They live in locked and vertical gated communities. Sadly, *gated* is the key word here and *community* is a misnomer. Lots slated for affordable housing have sat empty for thirty years. Why go after our buildings? Homes are not little boxes to park people in. Again, we wrote hundreds of letters, 170 people signed up to speak and on October 21, 2021, we fought against the plan that did not think co-ops deserve to remain in beautiful False Creek. In a city plagued with isolation and loneliness, we have to prioritize design that favours healthy, connected communities in spaces that inspire generosity. We have seen over and over how communities come together in emergencies better and faster than government can respond. (Rebecca Solnit documents that well.[54]) The best governments can do is support communities better.

Though they remain visionary and offer an enviable solution to the housing crisis, co-ops are an endangered species. All levels of government should protect them, especially in such an unaffordable city in Canada. But Hulchanski says:

> Canada's housing system, unlike that of most Western nations, relies almost exclusively on the market mechanism for the provision, allocation and maintenance of housing. This is a problem for households too poor to pay market rents for appropriate housing. These households generate a "social need" for housing rather than a "market demand" for it. A housing system based on the market mechanism cannot respond to social need.[55]

Most households are now too poor to pay current market rents; rents have unhinged themselves from working people's incomes.

The deals the city makes with developers for "affordable" housing seem pitifully inadequate and result in a few floors here and there to fill small quotas. This contributes to the insidious process of segregation and to poor doors and poor floors. At the same time, the city scrambles to build subsidized housing for the homeless and unhoused, much of which is pitifully inadequate for human living, let alone thriving. Some of the subsidized housing projects are not to die for but more to die in. More people are squeezed into, and depending on, modular and single room occupancy housing. What's more, the upzoning that happens after the city has sold land gives developers—who have sat on it for decades—windfall profits. The deals made for affordable housing often end up as one long process of developers trying to wiggle their way out of them over time. In a system set up to serve the market, where people feel alienated and unwelcome, co-ops take care of their members, address social justice issues and respond to social need.

When did we abandon creating liveable cities to focus entirely on sellable square footage of floor space? I devoted my summer to a steep learning curve to understand what was happening to housing beyond our neighbourhood. The movie *Push* (produced by Fredrik Gurten and starring Leilani Farah, former United Nations rapporteur for affordable housing) targets the financialization (commodification) of housing around the world.[56] Blackstone has become the largest global real estate equity firm. In a YouTube video that has since been taken down, the founder explains how the 2008 crisis allowed them to purchase 50,000 single family homes and profit from the misfortune of homeowners:

> You look for where the large pool of assets will be sold at big discounts and it was pretty obvious it was single family homes. Let's spend $25,000 or so fixing them up and then let's rent them out and make income producing assets out of them. Like an apartment business but not in just one large complex. And do it on a big enough scale.[57]

Should we have bailed out homeowners instead of finance? Lots of home-wrecker copycats followed.

Tax havens were a small shady corner of the world economy. Now, they are financial actors with much political power. It's not uncommon for them to be advisors to governments. They are likely there when stimulus packages get voted in. Blackstone invested heavily to obstruct rent control in California. They are hiding in plain sight and not paying their share of taxes. Governments are in danger of being complicit in criminal finance. In Canada, public policy since the mid-1980s has contributed to homelessness, argues Hulchanski, and has exacerbated the inequity in the rental housing sector.[58] The "hot" housing market during the pandemic contributed to British Columbia's economic growth. Perhaps this also explains why the government might be reluctant to regulate the market. You might be surprised who owns the buildings you rent. Map your neighbourhood.

The pandemic likely caused another round of evictions. Blackstone is on another shopping spree. As Europe tightens their housing policies to discourage such practices, they move to countries like ours. Renovictions, which sometimes turn violent, are the business model of this "industry." You might be participating through your pension plan. The International Union of Operating Engineers Local 115 pension plan owns two tower buildings that hold a housing community co-op, affordable housing in the city of Burnaby.[59] They want to sell the buildings to the highest bidder even though they have a generous offer, which will secure the housing remains in the affordable housing pool. A third of the people in these buildings are pensioners on fixed incomes. Consider the irony. Taking more affordable housing out of the market that seniors can use for the sake of returns on pensions seniors count on. People who are paying into these pensions have no idea how their fellow seniors are impoverished at the expense of returns on their pension plan numbers. Can the stewards of these pensions be more ethically minded? Can they find a way not to contribute to the tragedy of insecure and unaffordable housing? What will a win-win solution look like? Offering housing to seniors will be a better way to take care of them than counting on the dollars that will deflate in their portfolios by the time they get to them. Can they support pensioners while also protecting the assets of the people that pay into the pension plan? When we do that to gold, says Leilani Farah, it's not a human rights issue; using our homes to extract wealth is.[60] Old and connected communities are destroyed and replaced with luxury condo towers. What attracts finance to an area—its vibrancy and life—is exactly what is lost when the place turns into ghostly real estate deposit boxes. Financialization of housing is the graveyard for our homes; it's the new mining industry. This is not gentrification, more like zombification—a land grab that displaces people from their communities. People make places interesting, not concrete and glass. Estimates from a report that seems to be a first from 2019 say $7.4 billion have been laundered in British Columbia alone.[61] We could comfortably say it is likely a lot more than that as we do not have a way to keep track of illicit money. That is the whole point of such money. We refuse to compete with criminal money.

As millions of people are evicted, the numbers fall disproportionately along racial divides. We are suffering a system whose vagaries drift further from ethical and moral constraints and shorten the distance between crises. Hulchanski reminds us:

> It is important to understand that homelessness is not a "natural" phenomenon. It is the outcome of "normal"—that is, socially sanctioned—practices and activities that are intended to achieve government goals, maintain well-established institutions or allow certain enterprises to flourish. In other words, it is a by-product of Canada's housing system.[62]

Ironically, there is a demand for co-operative housing. Co-ops have very long waiting lists. The market remains uninterested. *The market will take care of it* is another myth we seem to live by. "None of us anticipated it would go on this long," my neighbour Maria Roth said. "We're aging in committee, not aging in community. Living here shouldn't be like winning the lottery."

To calculate the cost of return on this problematic False Creek South plan, the real estate department hired a private consultant. That information was not public. How can we gauge if the metrics that decide the course of our lives and define how and where we live is adequate for the challenges we face?

When a correspondent from *CityHallWatch*, a non-profit website focussed on city issues in Vancouver, made a freedom of information request on how the revered "return of cost" was calculated in the Shape Your City document, "Streamlining Rental: Making it Easier to Build Secure Rental Housing in More

Neighbourhoods," they received the following answer: "the city does not have the documents you are requesting in our care and custody."[63] Why, you ask?

> The city contracted an external subject matter expert to perform detailed financial viability testing in support of this work in which the consultant calculated and reported on expected return on cost. A complete detailed inventory of all the assumptions were not part of the deliverables of the contract.[64]

That might explain why we saw no numbers either. Does this also explain why senior city staff don't seem to be able to answer questions? Words come out of their mouths, not answers. Let's call it bafflegab. Even more troubling is that staff who do not have the numbers are advising our councillors who will be voting on the questionable plan. Just remediating the polluted soil on False Creek will be very costly and I am willing to bet a developer will not be undertaking that expense. We are just beginning to talk about the engineering aspect of water rising and structural viability of the area. That is a good few years job. Our leases cannot wait. We need them signed today. No bank will lend us money if we do not have at least a thirty-year amortization runway.

The market will not solve the housing problem but governments can close loopholes and update laws and regulations, and they also have the right of first refusal when "distressed assets" come up on the market. A simple rent control of five to ten years will discourage such practices that count on eviction for returns on investment to people who never have to worry about making rent.

It took three days for all of us to speak. Our councillors listened and voted in amendments to the short-sighted plan. We won this round. The report is going to the urban planning department. But our new chief urban planner came from Dallas three years ago, has little connection to the place we call home and admits she knows little about co-ops. All this continues to erode our trust. After three years, she was no longer in that position but we are left to reckon with the Broadway plan she oversaw.

We remain cautiously optimistic and very vigilant. We need a plan that "protects existing housing alongside the growth of co-op and non-profit housing as a priority—not an afterthought," to quote again my bright and dedicated neighbour Maria Roth. In March 2024, there was a motion from a councillor that raised our hopes. But it is March 2025 now and they are still changing the people who are working with us on the False Creek file. More of the same? More bafflegab?

Urban design defines how we interact as well as how we segregate rich from middle- and lower-income earners and people from nature. Syrian architect Dr. Marwa Al-Sabouni cautions how segregation into ghettoes can foster and fester conflict: In her book *The Battle for Home* she speaks of cities, and neighbourhoods not just as structures, but containers for our memories and our histories, intricately interwoven with our identities. She links modern architecture in her hometown as a factor in exacerbating the brutal war. "To destroy one's home should be taken as an equal crime to destroying one's soul."[65] This is what we should be worried about. Al-Sabouni draws a direct connection between how we build our cities and how we are with each other in a striking observation: "The undoing of the urban fabric has advanced hand in hand with the undoing of the moral fabric."[66] In a following book, *Building for Hope,*[67]

Al-Sabouni lays out a way we can build to foster peace: by making sure our built environments are planned in ways that alleviate five fears: fear of death, need, treachery, loneliness, and boredom. We need spaces that are welcoming and inspire generosity. This is what our neighbourhood does. We were successful in this fight because we have a community that trusts itself. We trust each other.

After years of reading and trying to understand this complex problem, to stay sane, I wrote a poetry book on the topic. *SCAR/CITY* is coming out in the same year as this book.[68] In a world of growing polarization and conflict, co-ops are places people choose to belong.

I invested many hours into these community work spaces, and for a very good reason. The enthusiasm and commitment are contagious. Many hands make light work and we continue to build more community to sustain the work. Each time I feel depleted or on the edge, someone comes along and gives me a boost with their effort and contributions. I am renewed and remind myself what all this amounts to. I keep a few choice quotes on my wall to also remind me what is possible when futility visits or despondence strikes. One of these quotes is from Jane Jacobs: "Historically, solutions to city problems have very seldom come from the top. They come from people who understand the problems first-hand because they're living with them and they have new, ingenious and often very offbeat ideas of how to solve them."[69] Urban design has to create conditions for belonging, which creates conditions for peace.

It Begins with Our Words

Note: the seven bolded words in this essay are words the Trump administration banned in official Human Services and Centers for Disease Control and Prevention documents in December 2017.[70]

After the September Uprising in 1923, deemed to be the first anti-fascist uprising, poet Geo Milev writes the epic long poem, "September." It describes the bloody, uneven battle between the well-armed and trained government army and the poorly armed workers and peasants. It speaks of the horrors, the sacrifices and the bravery of a people who rose up to fight against oppression. The poem makes the government squirm and they sentence Geo Milev, barely thirty years old, to a year in prison. The next day, he is called into the police station for a small "clarification" from which he never returns. Decades later, his skull, with its glass eye, is found in a mass grave near Sofia. He lost his eye on the front lines but lost his life for writing a poem.

There are many dark periods in Bulgarian history, not the least disturbing of which is when thousands from the intelligentsia disappeared without a trace. In Bulgaria, the poets, writers and intellectuals were often also the revolutionaries and the first to be targeted.

As much as I want to think of this as something of the past, attacks on books and words and the untimely deaths of writers, journalists and revolutionaries are still plaguing us. In 2007, a car bomb exploded on Al-Mutanabbi Street in Baghdad—the historic centre of Baghdad booksellers. Dozens lost their lives and at least a hundred were injured. It mobilized us writers to respond with *Al-Mutanabbi Street Starts Here,* an anthology of poetry.

In 2014, the poetry community mourned Arab Iranian poet Hashem Shaabani, executed by the order of Iranian President Hassan Rouhani. Shaabani fought for human rights and was sentenced to death under the charge that he was "waging war on God" with his poetry.[71]

The mind-boggling purge that began in 2016 under the reign of Turkish President Recep Tayyip Erdoğan has affected the justice system, education, government employees, the military, police and media. "According to the P24 press freedom group, there are more than 160 journalists behind bars in Turkey, most of whom were arrested under the state of emergency imposed after the coup attempt."[72]

As I write this, Jamal Khashoggi, a prominent Saudi journalist and columnist for the *Washington Post,* has been missing for over two weeks. It's presumed he was assassinated in the Saudi Arabian embassy in Turkey while trying to sort out paperwork for his marriage. A critic of the regime, he left his country when he knew it was no longer safe for him to do his work there.

Books matter. In 2022, author Salman Rushdie was stabbed on stage while giving a lecture at an educational centre in western New York. This happened years after his book *The Satanic Verses* was banned in many countries and the leader of Iran issued a *fatwa* calling for his death. Words matter. That is why they are a threat to such regimes. They throw the proverbial monkey wrench in their story.

Narges Mohammadi won the 2023 Nobel Peace Prize, though she was absent for the presentation because she was in jail. She was awarded the prize "for her fight against the oppression of women in Iran and her fight to promote human rights and freedom for all."[73] Even more recently, we witnessed the concerted and sustained effort to eliminate Alexei Navalny, who was a prominent critic of Vladimir Putin. Multiple attempts to assassinate him are documented in Daniel Roher's 2022 documentary *Navalny*, which won an Oscar.[74] The cause of his death in a prison in Russia's far north in 2024 remains inconclusive.

It's not surprising that when fundamentalist and totalitarian regimes come into power the first thing they go after is language. Our poets, scientists, journalists, artists, activists and intellectuals have always been in danger under such governments, often dying for their words alone. These regimes can only work if they control the narrative.

We live at a time where **entitlement** trumps **diversity**, when *truth* is a self-serving convenience, a time when government can get away with *alternative* facts. It's a world where **evidence-based** and **science-based** narratives compete with money, conspiracy theories, extremist cults and views, where corporate-serving narratives are manufactured on a whim. Inconvenient books and stories can be banned or burned. Inconvenient people and whistleblowers are punished or, worse, dispensed with. People argue over easy-to-prove facts. We seem to have left the age of information and walked straight into the age of misinformation, some call post-truth. Many of us are still in the age of how-is-this-even-possible. It's not just possible; it has happened before.

In an article published on *Ceasefire*, an independent political and cultural publication, Andy McLaverty Robinson discusses

Walter Benjamin's analysis of the effects of economic crisis on everyday life in Germany: how the inherently flawed nature of capitalism leads to conflict and how the Second World War was likely a solution to that problem—the problem of over-production which people who are not getting paid adequate wages cannot resolve.[75] Capitalism is not only in a crisis, it needs crisis after crisis to keep itself going and it appears wars are a way out of the crisis.

For decades, the United States has been solving uncompromising financial crises by finding someone to blame, and going to war seems to be the way it deals with its economic problems. That seems to appease markets and even people. For a little while. If you produce weapons, you have to have markets to sell them in. If there's no need, you create one by starting a war somewhere. This is the simple debilitating logic of the tragic drama of supply and demand, of profits divorced from morals, and being only accountable to shareholders. How is a system like that threatened? Truth can be that monkey wrench thrown in its workings, which makes it sputter, stall, sows doubt. But today, we see multiple narratives, a lot of money behind some of them and more wrenches in the air.

One thing that neo-liberalism has had a hard time facing is that its ideology and politics can lead to fascism. We currently see these tendencies played out in a different guise. According to Benjamin, war seems to be the convenient (or inevitable) outcome when there is no will to address the root causes of the real issue, which is: "challenging the property system."[76] War, however, can channel those grievances of the masses. But to go to war, you need to have a bulletproof story. Or at least one that is immune to monkey wrenches. In the Bush Junior years, we witnessed how it's not easy to find the right lies or the right metaphors to fire up a nation to go to war. But after a few tries, and a whole lot of lies, they did. If someone came to you today and told you that your economic system is designed around an unpredictable crisis after crisis, crash, burn and trash philosophy, which can only lead to war, would you sign up for it? The world cannot afford this kind of brute and ignorant problem solving. Not anymore.

In an article in the *New York Times*, Jason Stanley speaks of how totalitarian propaganda is based on narratives that are easy to grasp, narratives which explain people's grievances, narratives which blame minority groups for these grievances. These narratives aim to distort reality and assert the leader's power. Though this distortion, Stanley claims, is also its biggest weakness.[77]

Does that sound painfully familiar? We upgrade our computer software regularly but don't take much care of our delicate mental software. It's hard to deny that we're gullible and susceptible to manipulation, especially given the right conditions of indignity, poverty, insecurity or incentive. We live in spaces that are increasingly surveilled and monitored. If your world is manufactured, your truth can be too. It's then a stone's throw from there to limiting yourself to a group of people who only think like you and fear what is unfamiliar or other. Should we be surprised, then, that alternative narratives have moved in from the fringes and have been sweeping across the United States like the wildfires we are also battling? No, we should not be surprised. It has happened before. But we are shocked anew at how fragile democracy can be.

It is a lot easier to feed us simple stories than rethinking how to redistribute obscene accumulation of wealth, and address the true causes of our discontent and depravity. Such accumulation of wealth is at odds with democracy. At that point democracy becomes an inconvenience for the uber rich and parts ways from their idea of "freedom." (Update as of early 2025: Trump was elected for a second time in November 2024 and threatens tariffs and annexation of Canada. A whole page of disappearing words was published in the *New York Times* within the first two months, among these words are: *women, identity, belonging, multicultural, female, equity, hate speech, social justice,* to name a few.[78]) Of course, this is hard for the rational brain to comprehend. That is the point. At a time when there are so many competing narratives out there, the grip on our minds and attention is more taxing and debilitating than ever.

When we read a novel or watch a play, it creates a reality in which the actions of the characters make sense. The writer has to be consistent to gain the reader's trust. The reader has to suspend disbelief to participate fully. That's the contract we enter when we read fiction for the sake of art, entertainment or to relate it to our lives. In advertising, we are clear what underlies the ad. We know we are being told a story for the purpose of being sold a thing. That is why advertising to children is so insidious and is, or at least was, banned in countries like Sweden. Studies show that children are unable to separate the actual program from the commercials shown in between segments. I did not grow up with commercials and felt that dissonance first-hand. My brain tries to integrate the first few frames of the commercial before it switches gears and recognizes it's a commercial. When we do that in politics, it is even more problematic. When it comes to government propaganda, it is not clear what kind of contract we enter. And when lies are not a deterrent, then you can present any narrative to assert your power. Our storied minds delight in what makes sense to us, what is consistent and what orders and simplifies the world to make it more bearable.

Capitalism gone global through the multinational corporation is a hard story to sell. It is a ghost story[79]; it takes a big machine to create it and it takes a lot of suspending of disbelief to buy into it. There is enough dissonance and enough people willing to spin a narrative tailored to the ruling administration. We forget there is a big-money machine underpinning this propaganda. And now that we are all forced to connect through social media algorithms, this machine is more powerful than ever. With the sheer speed of spreading misinformation, it has become its own war machine. In his speech at the 2024 Vancouver Writers Fest, Timothy Snyder reminded us: "Computer screens tend to make us more predictable; books tend to make us less predictable."[80]

Felipe Fernandez-Armesto says in his book *Truth*: "There is no social order without trust, and no trust without truth or, at least, agreed truth finding procedures."[81] What happens to our mental health, to our communities and even families when we're bombarded with bits of contradictory information, when competing narratives pull us in different directions? Is this our latest version of the tower of Babel? In a world dissociated from the world, you can push hate and manufactured worlds like cheap street drugs. What we take to be true, what we believe and what we perceive have fragile and tenuous threads. Each can influence the other. And each can shift depending on the environment. That becomes easier if you make the real world unbearable. "When people stop believing in something, they do not believe in nothing; they believe in anything," says Fernandez-Armesto.[82] We forget too quickly what has already happened because even our memory is compromised in our screen-infested, immediate-gratification "reality." But we also forget that authoritarian rhetoric attempts to "convey power by defining reality. The reality they offer is very simple. It is offered with the goal of switching voters' value systems to the authoritarian value system of the leader."[83] Often, that includes creating an enemy of the people and building up fear. "If we have different values and different facts," Snyder said, "we cannot do anything together."[84]

To add to the complexity and madness, social media reinforces this narrowing into echo chambers. We keep thinking of artificial intelligence as something romantic and sexy but the unpredicted outcomes of algorithms, let loose without human oversight, are already running our lives and altering our very soft brain software. It reduces us to reptilian impulses and attacks. It reduces us, too, to an algorithm. People we disagree with, who challenge us and whose views do not align with ours are a click away from being unfriended, dispensed with, blocked. Social media mobs and trolls can reduce you to a label in record time, drag you through the hate-speech dirt (under the guise of "free speech," of course) and virtually crucify you. It's hard to go down the trash chute of people's opinions. It breeds fear to speak your mind. God forbid if you are **transgender**, visibly different in skin colour or religion, or you are a group that is used as a tool to create fear and labelled the enemy of the people. If you live in an echo chamber, you become an echo chamber. This isn't just old and boring, it's dangerous. And we are witnessing more and more the kind of dangerous it is. Even more grievous is that we are robbed of the attention we need to be devoting to envisioning a better future. Amusing ourselves to death (as Neil Postman writes in his book *Amusing Ourselves to Death*[85]) is also an oppression and suppression we buy into, this one willingly. We are seduced by it and we are at our most **vulnerable** when we participate in it.

Thankfully, people know when enough is enough. In 1968, in the iconic riots in Paris, students at University Paris Nanterre and Sorbonne University stood up for their rights and began a revolution that moved beyond its initial demands. More importantly, they opened up spaces for conversations that couldn't be had before. It became necessary to find common ground between students and administration, workers and government. Community isn't just something we feel we need; it's a powerful survival mechanism, a place of sanity and humanity. Community is not a luxury. It's good for us to be **vulnerable** with each other, to trust each other and count on each other. It's good for our brains. What despotic, tyrannical and totalitarian regimes are after is to splinter that trust to control better. They ritualize violence until it makes sense. They make a spectacle out of it. These aren't new developments. Yet many of us are still curled up in the **fetus** phase of how-is-this-even-possible. I keep saying to myself: *Anytime now, I'll find out this is some black comedy, a farce, a theatre of the absurd I can go home from*. But it isn't.

In 1990, I was a student in a master's program in English philology. We occupied Sofia University and demanded the resignation of then-President Petar Mladenov. Even though Mladenov helped topple the totalitarian ruler Todor Zhivkov and remove the Communist party's guaranteed right to rule, people felt he continued with the same old politics. After he was caught on camera saying he would bring in the tanks against the tens of thousands of anti-government demonstrators, the students asked for his resignation. I remember being in a chanting crowd so closely packed my body swayed when the crowd swayed. We were one organism moving in unison. A cardboard tank, erected in the courtyard of the university, symbolized what Mladenov at first denied he had said. More importantly, we demanded democratic change. The occupation of the university went on for at least a month, though in my memory it felt much longer.

The support we got was more than inspiring. There were lectures and discussions with visiting experts. Artists and theatre actors came to show their support with performances and talks. Professors camped out in solidarity with the students. People brought us food, passing it to us through the bars in the courtyard fence. Eventually, our demands were met. In other parts of the world, students haven't been as lucky. (Update: in the past year, university campuses became the places for students to rally against blatant violation of human rights. This is not for or against one people; it is what we owe each other. Now that, too, is in danger of being criminalized.)

When corporate and political corruption begins to weigh unbearably on citizens, something has to give in. Political shakeups in Bulgaria seem to come about through actions by optimistic, fed-up youth looking into the muzzle of their impoverished future. The power of places of knowledge cannot be undermined; they are usually at the head of change and revolutions. That is why they are also the first to be targeted.

In 2018, survivors of the high school shooting in Parkland, Florida, led the March for Our Lives demanding gun control. They were disregarded, dismissed by the first Trump administration, whose policies have the pungent and sickening odour of disregard for the rule of law and truth. This, of course, is a foreboding sign for the government. It doesn't help that the warped and compromised nature of *Fox "News"* goes to unconscionable lengths to pollute the airwaves and poison susceptible minds. As I write these words, there is a shooting in a synagogue in Pittsburgh. My Facebook wall again turned into a long lament of grief, dismay, disbelief: *How is this even possible?* Many more victims have been recorded since. In the past three years, the Ukraine war and the decimation of Palestine have filled our screens and conversations.

Student protests proliferated far and wide.

We have come to the edge of hyper-predatory capitalist greed, a neo-liberal agenda gone haywire, an agenda that cannot face the consequences of its beliefs and actions. In his book *Technofeudalism*, Yanis Varoufakis suggests we name things for what they are.[86] That way, we know how to deal with them better. According to him, what we know as capitalism has now morphed into "technofeudalism." Where money is god, even the god of religion is subservient to the money god. Does it feel like these gods are shaking hands and making deals under the table? You can bring your gun to church. You can get a discount on Wednesdays for bringing your concealed carry permit for your pistol at Just the Cook houseboat restaurant in Panama City, Florida. We cannot afford to think the market is wise anymore or that predatory capital has any ethical or social justice concerns. Its bottom line is profit. Nobel Prize–winning economist Joseph E. Stiglitz says, "Milton Friedman gave them an economic argument for why they should be unconcerned about morality. After a third of a century of this experiment, we now know that it is wrong and that you can make money by destroying the world. And there is something wrong with that."[87]

We also cannot afford to think that this is some act of God. It isn't. The idea of a government calling for less government seems to be a paradox in itself. It is a government that no longer serves the people but serves some chosen people. For such people, democracy is at odds with their idea of freedom. So, when the uber rich speak of freedom, they are not thinking of us nor do they mean democracy. Adam Smith's invisible hand is no longer invisible. It is a meddling greedy hand that keeps adjusting the dials to please shareholders. Recently, I encountered Stiglitz saying: "The reason that Adam Smith's invisible hand often seems invisible is that it is not there."[88] You do not have to be an economist to see through this myth.

There is only so much you can push a system or a people before it reveals its terrible flaws, the many ways it has devised of impoverishing its citizens, its communities, by tampering with their food and water, language and culture, land and environment and, of late, their homes, health care and public funding. Too much is invested in the same old ways; the system and its old ways hold tooth, claw and nail. It creates schizophrenic narratives to defend those investments and institutions at any cost. If people turned off the TV and started talking to each other, their communities would be better off and their local governments would not be so gutted and impotent.

What happens to trust in times like these? Greed and agreed-upon truth aren't going to make friends under the current ideology because it has to tell itself lies to keep going or exclude obvious facts in order to sustain its premises. "Factuality is not the same thing as information," Snyder said. "We are bombarded with information... Factuality has to involve local circumstances, local conditions... Factuality takes a lot of effort. It has to be worked at."[89]

A much longer time ago, even Plato foresaw what we cannot believe. In *The Republic,* he juxtaposes fortune and virtue in an oligarchy: "The more they think of making a fortune, the less they think of virtue; for when riches and virtue are placed together in the scales of the balance, the one always rises as the other falls."[90] Plato goes on to talk about what happens when wealth is the main qualification for the job, as if he predicted the Trump government 2.0: "Just think what happens if pilots were to be chosen according to their property and a poor man were refused permission to steer, even though he were a better pilot?"[91] The defects of a system like that are blatantly obvious. Still, the United States re-elected a brand name for a president (one of poor character and temper who also has now been convicted). We do not have enough room in this book to list the felonies and counts. Not winning the seat for president likely would have sent him to jail.

How do we balance the scales? Plato is not a prophet giving us prophecies; he just thought deeply about human nature and its propensities. In Book VIII of *The Republic,* Plato discusses the transition from democracy to tyranny as if it's as natural and inevitable a process as the seasons changing.

It's also paradoxical to want certain rights and freedoms while denying them to another group of people. We get George Orwell's *Animal Farm* all over again. We cannot but draw parallels to *1984,* his dystopian science fiction novel with the doublethink and newspeak. The Greek rhetorician, Isocrates, saw the pitfalls of taking freedom irresponsibly: democracy is not insolence, liberty is not lawlessness, equality is not impudence of speech and happiness is not a licence to do what you please. Yet we see how these traits have flared under the encouragement of an amoral government. Snyder called such self-obsession, an individual thinking only of oneself, "negative freedom."[92] None of this is new to the world yet we act like it is.

We have only recently begun to deal with the shameful episode of residential schools here in Canada and to recognize that we live on a great number of traditional Indigenous Territories. It was 2014 when, finally, our city council unanimously voted to formally acknowledge this fact and gaping oversight. It reads: "Underlying all other truths spoken during the Year of Reconciliation is the truth that the modern city of Vancouver was founded on the traditional territories of the Musqueam, Squamish and

Tsleil-Waututh First Nations and that these territories were never ceded through treaty, war or surrender."[93]

Unfortunately, the commodification of our housing through the current un–real estate is a disease that has infested our homes, mining them for profit. The only reason this is possible is because, long ago, someone decided they can sell the land that is not theirs to private owners. The wealth of the United States and Canada and many other places is based on this theft premise, this crime. Neither the City of Vancouver nor the Government of Canada has done much since to show that this land is not for sale or, if it is, it will benefit those that were wronged to begin with. At the time of writing, thousand-year-old trees are being logged as fast as possible despite the Fairy Creek protest and barricades, where our young and old are being treated like criminals and assaulted by law enforcement to sustain the narrative.

The world moves forward, however, and, if history teaches us anything, sooner or later, enough people see through the propaganda and the fabricated narratives, the strategy of altering and controlling one's reality—and eventually citizens will stand up in enough numbers that their voices will be hard to ignore. And it begins with our words. But it takes an awful lot longer once we erode our democratic checks and balances.

To summon what the inimitable Ursula K. Le Guin said in her speech at the National Book Awards in 2014: "We live in capitalism, its power seems inescapable—but then, so did the divine right of kings. Any human power can be resisted and changed by human beings. Resistance and change often begin in art. Very often in our art, the art of words."[94] If capitalism is leaving at the expense of a worse deal, then what? If according to Varoufakis what killed capitalism is technofeudalism, what will it take to kill technofeudalism? Long ago, the internet was a place of hope, a promise for the creation of a commons, but "the internet shattered capitalism's evolutionary fitness... it did incubate a new form of capital, which has ultimately empowered its owners to break free of capitalism and become a whole new ruling class of their own."[95] These are the technofeudalists who now can control our words too.

So, when a corporation or a government today begins to control language, especially if that person or group is in position of power, there's no time to waste. We cannot afford to *not* pay attention. Especially if you live in a country where free speech is still flaunted as a right, you not only have to take responsibility for what comes out of your mouth but also for what cannot. It's time to fight for your right to keep that right and explicitly define the responsibilities we have to abide by with the right to free speech. *The right to swing your arm ends where my nose begins.* The right to say what you want ends where my dignity and humanity is violated.

Le Guin is no longer with us, but her words are. So are Geo Milev's words, and Hashem Shaabani's words, and Navalny's words, and the thousands of others who have stood up for humanity and freedom and fought in the service of human rights and dignity. Sooner or later, the scales will have to be balanced. Any government or corporate feudal lord worth their salt should take heed—or start preparing for its own demise.

What Is the Purpose of Your Trip?

Of Ghosts Past and Present

What is the purpose of your trip? asked the visa application I filled out months ago. *Business or pleasure*? I picked pleasure and immediately had a strange sense I didn't know what that meant. I've checked the box before but this time I meant it. Usually, it stood in for *none of your business*. I was going to travel with a friend on the longest plane ride ever to a place I've never been to. We were flying from Vancouver to Tokyo, then Tokyo to Ho Chi Minh City. We paid for a week-long, all-inclusive yoga retreat in Mui Ne; bought opera tickets and booked a street-food tour and hotel in Ho Chi Minh City; and purchased internal flights to De Nang. But my own two legs were going nowhere. I spent the three hours before takeoff at a check-in counter. That's as far as I got on my trip to Vietnam.

Travelling just-for-pleasure was a novel concept. Travel was always for a reason: moving, immigrating, family visits, changing jobs, conferences or book launches. Vacations meant transitions, sometimes momentous change. Travel meant work but not the kind that fits in the business category.

A few years ago, I stopped flying to conferences. I had to pay for registration, flights, room and board without funding support. I wasn't getting paid to present, it was not environmentally sound and I was not partaking of the place. When I flew to a small town in England for the Poetic Inquiry Symposium, I remember the oaks creaking as we walked to the conference venue, the urgent surf at night, the purple figs from the corner grocery store, the way the sun fell in the room in the morning. I remember reading Rilke out loud the night we arrived; it transported us more fully to the old continent. But I do not remember much from the town or the people, except the arm that yanked me out of the way from stepping in front of a fast car on a narrow winding road. I was looking the wrong way. Thank you to that person, and their arm. In Montreal, I only remember the awkward arrangements at the Airbnb. Negotiating the curtained privacy, or lack of privacy, took up the little free time we had. These are whirlwind experiences. I yearn now to commune with the spirit of Montreal: the place people thought I came from when I moved to Canada.

Was I ever a tourist? I grew up between continents. In our back-and-forths, we visited countries. In England, I was terrified in the dungeons beneath the Tower of London. We walked in Hyde Park by ourselves. When my sister and I got lost in the Natural History Museum, it was nothing compared to losing her in a bustling Italian market. In Egypt, we climbed inside a pyramid. I remember sitting on a camel. The hotel hallways were so curved I was scared to go to the bathroom. I left a camisole over our room's lampshade, which burned a hole through it. In Madrid, we strolled through the Prado Museum, the images of Goya still lodged in my impressionable mind. The bulls fighting at the corrida de toros were clearly on the losing end; we watched each one dragged out of the arena after the spectacled ritual slaughter. We stayed up to watch flamenco till way past midnight; the city came to life after our bedtime. My parents believed this type of travel was good education for us kids. And it was. We followed them from country to country. Sometimes, they regretted taking us along—especially the time we flooded our hotel room in Italy.

As an adult I couldn't afford to travel much, let alone for pleasure. I made sure I secured maximum enjoyment from each trip, despite the work. I packed as many reasons into a trip as I could. I learned to be present amidst the work, challenge and effort. Over time, I learned to secure time each day to breathe deeply and compose myself. A way of leaving and coming back stronger, without the exhaustion of travel. A way to be briefly outside the regiment of the ticking clock. Time travelling of sorts—or shall we say out-of-time travel.

The words *tourist* and *tourism* were already in use in the late 1700s and early 1800s. They came from the word *tour,* within which is folded the Latin *tornare,* "to turn on a lathe." The ancient Greek *tornos* (τόρνος) means "lathe." Presumably, it was due to the circular nature of leaving and coming back to the same place. For me, the image captures how I feel as a tourist: I am the one spinning on the lathe at the mercy of businesses shaping my experience. Or shall I say Xperience, where the poetry of travel gets lost. I had never thought of how one defines a tourist, but Valene L. Smith in *Hosts and Guests* defines a tourist as "a temporarily leisured person who voluntarily visits a place away from home for the purpose of experiencing a change."[96] Perhaps I was never that kind of *leisured*?

When my kids were about five and eight, we visited my parents in Bulgaria. For my birthday, they surprised me with an all-inclusive trip to a small Greek resort. They looked after their grandkids while we went on vacation. How normal that sounded, a "normal" we'd not experienced much as a couple. The most fun I had on that bus tour was the time on the beach. The next day, while the rest of the group went to Meteora monasteries, we snuck back to the beach. After what felt like forever hours on a bus getting there, I couldn't imagine getting on another bus for another six hours to Meteora and back with a bunch of tired and hungover tourists. I sincerely regret not seeing the Byzantine monasteries. Perched on the cliffs between Earth and heaven, they are undoubtedly one of the wonders of the world. But I don't regret spending the day on the beach with silky white pebbles; the music they made when the water rushed back through them still *ush-sh-sh-sh-es* through my head. The barista who made my coffee made it just the way I like it. It cost the same but the care was palpable. Mount Olympus startled me each time I looked over my shoulder. It doesn't rise as high as it does in the myths. I can see why the gods picked this place. It reminds me of Vitosha on the outskirts of the city where I was born. Are the gods *still* there? Or did tourists kick them out of their abode? Did *they* ever feel at home? Mostly, we interacted with other dazed tourists or people who were versed in the business of herding and managing tourists.

On our return, my father wanted to know what I thought of the Meteora monasteries. I confessed we skipped that leg of the tour. His face was a combination of shock and disappointment. I'd failed him again. Sorry, Dad, I'm just not made of tourist material.

As we planned for Vietnam, it was hard to ignore the feeling that prevented me from getting excited. I gave up travelling alone when I was twenty-four. I've yet to visit the Isle of Skye. I'd travelled so much on my own at that point, I drew the line there. In my early twenties, I hitchhiked with friends through multiple countries that didn't require visas. If we met today, we'd have stories to tell, laugh and reminisce about. That was meaningful to me. I could get excited about travelling with a friend. Building memories with others is a country I want to live in.

It was time I shut up about this ominous feeling. We booked the flights and proceeded to obtain visas. I put my life on hold for three weeks. That was more work than I realized. We spent months planning and preparing.

Except, I could not get on the plane.

At the check-in counter, we discovered a typo on my entry visa to Vietnam in the middle of my middle name. In other words, my family name. In the place of the *N* there was a *V*. It was not too misspelled. This looked like an honest mistake. But even an honest mistake can cause headaches. Much was contingent on that one piece of paper. I avoid using my middle name to spare myself the misspellings. When Elections Canada misspelled it, they misspelled the *v* as an *r*. You can see how a handwritten *v* can look like an *r*. An honest mistake. I only brought it up at election time, trusted it would get fixed before the next election. Changing it only took a few election cycles.

Japan Airlines did not issue me a boarding pass due to such a benign error. If I was dealing with a machine, the algorithm would prevent me from moving forward. But I was dealing with a human, not an algorithm. I go to humans because they can troubleshoot, solve problems creatively and, one hopes, compassionately. What was I dealing with here? What happens when people mimic algorithms? The cost of this typo had just become very steep for someone who works hard for her dollars.

My hopes were raised when the attendant, who was not issuing my boarding pass, pulled up a site on her phone and said, "If you hurry, you can get a 15MinuteVisa." My friend and I went to work on navigating the urgent visa site. On the first attempt (in all the haste), we didn't notice that the $65 USD I paid was only for a normal visa. I found that out only when I mentioned it to the staff. By now, they were getting painfully familiar with our story. One of them said, "That cannot be a 15MinuteVisa"; the other said, "The 15MinuteVisa is much more expensive." My story had fired up their pity, understanding and compassion. That was nice to have but not as nice as having that 15MinuteVisa. Back to the site.

This time, we were sure to check the tiny bullet point in front of the Urgent 15MinuteVisa. But the website refused my Visa credit card. I couldn't pay for the visa, which was now showing as $350 USD. After two more failed attempts to pay with my Visa for my urgent visa, we used my friend's Visa card. We'd settle accounts later. Right now, all we wanted was that 15MinuteVisa. We gave my friend's cell number. Clicked submit. And waited. I'd monitor email, she'd monitor the phone. It was 11:19 a.m. Our flight departed at 12:35 p.m.

Our hard-earned money travelled between currencies and countries. Swiftly. No problem. But I was going nowhere. During that time, the $350 USD turned into $500 CAD and close to $9 million Vietnamese dong (VND); the mistakenly paid $65 USD had translated to $93 CAD—over $1.5 million VND. These are rough numbers; who's counting cents when little made sense.

Fifteen minutes passed—an agonizing wait hemmed in with a bit of hope. Another fifteen minutes dragged by. At that point, my friend was urged to get through security and head to the departure gate. If there was a miracle, I'd follow. I was hoping I would, after all, be able to board and join her on that hard-earned window seat I booked us the day before.

Forty minutes passed. Then fifty. I watched the counters of Japan Airline get packed up and vacated. The monitor switched to the name of another airline. People lined up for the next flight. I lugged my freshly packed carry-on to the SkyTrain $600 CAD poorer. My original visa with the typo had cost me only $25 USD. I'd have paid more to make sure there was no typo.

I spent the rest of the day trying to figure out the faulty visa that had so far delivered zero pleasure. I'd done all the work, and some, but no one made it their business to secure the pleasure. Someone called my friend regarding the 15MinuteVisa application when she was on the plane waiting to take off. But it was too late.

When I got home, I had an email: "Have you applied for a visa with us before?" I thought that was a strange question when I already had a visa, albeit a faulty one. I told them my name was misspelled. They asked me to send the faulty visa. I wasn't sure why they didn't already have it. This was happening quickly between brief long-distance calls and one-liner emails. I insisted on getting my visa in case I could book another flight. They said: "We need your flight itinerary first." I said: "I just missed it; your 15MinuteVisa did not arrive in fifteen minutes." I don't want to buy another ticket unless I have a visa that works.

They persisted—they cannot issue a visa without an itinerary. After about twenty-five back-and-forth emails and a handful of long-distance calls, I did get a "visa" that "might" work. It came with instructions, the most unsettling one: a man will meet me at the airport. He'll be holding a sign with my name and get me through with no problem while I relax. Visas don't come with a man waiting for you at the airport. What did I pay for?

This was beginning to sound like a scam. I was getting spooked. It was past 4:00 p.m. I was hungry, exhausted and frustrated. Is that what being a tourist feels like? What bolstered me was the way both my sons responded. My younger son was in San Francisco on Skype with me while simultaneously on his phone cancelling as much as possible of the old flight. He finalized re-booking a new flight. When he had to go to a meeting, he passed the agent, Prince, he had worked with over to me. This intensified the surreal feeling of the day. I had recently talked to Michael Jackson who was trying to sell me some deal. My older son came home, put his head on my shoulder, a dear and rare gesture. He tried to trace the faulty visa origin and see if there was any recourse to that. Their mobilization and care were true gifts. By 5:00 p.m., I told my younger son to cancel the flight he had booked, which left at midnight that day. I had spoken to Jesus by then, too, who took over from Prince. This was already a lot more work (and expense) than I was willing to put into a trip just for pleasure. My intuition was working overtime, my body was depleted and begging me to give up. They both bypassed any resistance I could mount against them. I felt instant relief making that decision.

The next morning, there was another email from the now-suspect visa people. A different person had emailed me overnight on the same string of emails. It said: "DISCARD the visa in the last email. It will not work." I was to use the new attached visa. This one looked more like the faulty visa but was missing a QR code. I was even more relieved I had cancelled the flight that would have left three hours before that email was sent; my son only lost $150 USD instead of the full price of the ticket.

Could this fiasco explain the heavy feeling I'd had all along? The whispering was so strong about a month before departure that I woke up one morning in a panic: *If I don't go, will that mess up my friend's trip?* We had a quick call. She assured me she'd go regardless. That was a relief. I'm not sure she understood my strange premonition. At the time, she called it self-sabotage. No point pursuing this early in the morning, over the phone, in an alien-to-premonitions language. How to translate the ineffable? I comforted myself by attributing it to things people told me: *You are resisting change, you worry too much, stop worrying, just go have fun.* This told to someone who has moved between places all her life. My neighbour diagnosed: "Energetically, you did not want to go." Understanding this was going to be work; getting others to understand it even more work.

I called my sister. She had had a premonition at the beginning of 2024: a feeling she described as *thick and heavy as molasses.* We spoke for two hours. That year, she was let go after seven years serving as dean at the university with no explanation. She needed to make sense of that and a few other harrowing things. I encouraged her to write it out. To my surprise, she did. Spending time with my sister was another true gift in this ordeal. We made a good dent in catching up on quality time. She has been writing since.

Have we grown too arrogant and loud to listen to our inner barometers, these inner forecasting systems? If we haven't lost the skill to read them, do we have adequate words for the readings?

❦

I asked the now no-15MinuteVisa people for my money back. They said they gave me the 15MinunteVisa; it was my fault I didn't use it. "We are very confused about you have [sic] missed your second flight so now will explain 1 more time from the beginning for you." This was accompanied by a photo of someone holding my name on a sign: proof they did *their* part. Who was I communicating with? Each time I called, a different person picked up. Once, it sounded like I woke up a man; another time, the woman talking to me sounded as if she was amidst loud traffic. Much was getting lost in these translations. In the end, I got $70 USD back from the $350 USD I spent. I still owe my friend money. When the amounts were translated back to Canadian dollars, they were less than what I initially paid. Someone was making money while I was losing mine but getting nothing in return.

❦

I was going to leave this story at the airport but it pursued me. Things I thought I'd left behind came back to visit and haunt me. The helplessness before a piece of paper is debilitating. It's not your fault but you bear the consequences. Such helplessness can reduce one to tears, anger or both. But I was neither angry nor did I cry.

Had Japan Airlines let me board, I might've been able to figure out the visa fix on the spot. I've had to do that before. But I couldn't get to Vietnam to fix this error. It was their mistake, after all. I've hung on many such tenuous threads. Who should take responsibility?

Could the attendant have resolved this mistake? The employees at the airport told me this happens often. You'd think by now there would be a system to deal with it. Does hyper-connected technology help us solve problems better? Or is it eroding our agency further? Does it hamper us in new and innovative ways with each upgrade? Such familiar ghosts.

Would writing this liberate it into insight? What is this insight?

Two days before my departure, I went to my credit union to exchange Canadian dollars for American. Instead of directly exchanging to the local dong, I had to buy American dollars first. The bank teller and I got chatting. She said she was from Mexico.

I said, "I've always wanted to go to Mexico," then added, "But I'm sorry, I won't go to Mexico. I don't want to contribute to the tourist occupation there."

I panicked at what had just come out of my mouth. This was no small talk. One can think such things but it's different when you say them out loud. I was expressing my care in an unusual way. The moment froze.

Her eyes softened, she put her hand on her heart, and with a slight tip of her head, mouthed: "Thank you."

Time stopped. She surprised me too. She told me of a village split in two by train tracks. It cut the school off from the community. It was not safe for kids to cross the tracks daily. Asking for the school to be moved in the end resulted in the community having to apologize to those who bullied the tracks through their village. She counted my cash: $500 CAD became about $350 USD, which would roughly be $9 million VND.

Every transaction went through the American dollar. Ding dong. The American dollar has its nose in both your business and pleasure. The United States still has a tether on me. We said goodbye. Was this a foreshadowing of what ensued two days later? Here I was, going to go to Vietnam as a… tourist? I didn't have to go to Mexico to fall in love with its people.

Another ghost rose in conversations with family. It turns out my family name was altered generations before. My great-grandfather, who lived under the yoke of the Ottoman Empire, had his own merchant ship. He often passed through the Bosphorus Strait. When he lost his passport, the Turkish authorities reissued it but spelled his name Bunev (Бунев) instead of Buynov (Буйнов). Turkish does not have the й sound. My dad also told me of a place in Bulgaria called Буйново, which he is pretty sure was named after my great-great uncle. It huddles in the mountains; a winding road descends into the village. My great-grandfather's brother was part of the fight for liberation. I hope to visit the village and the museum one day, where this history lives.

What's in a name, after all? Changing someone's name is a disconnect from a familial community. It makes it harder to connect the dots on ancestral maps. I only had to deal with an entry visa (going nowhere). Such stakes are relatively low. I'll lose a good chunk of money, some sanity and all that promise for pleasure.

Watching myself pack revealed another insight: everything I packed was meaningful. As if I was packing a story, as if my carry-on would be a carefully curated home away from home. As if one can code a sense of permanence into things. I still sleep on the same mattress we bought when we got married. Initially, the bed was a full-set, solid oak, king-sized bed. In various moves, it shed. As the rooms shrank, so did the bed. The headboard went first, then the side tables, then the wood frame dropped out. Finally, the husband left. Now, it's just a mattress and box spring. This bed has survived seven moves and numerous milestones. It's the island I retreat to at the end of the day. I thought my resistance to getting a new bed was because I didn't want to drag into the house volatile toxic fumes of PVCs, formaldehyde, flame retardants and other chemicals emanating from new mattresses. But there was more: I surround myself with objects imbued with stories. I cherish being surrounded by people and objects that hold my stories and remind me where I come from. As everything changes around me, it seems crucial to keep some things the same. As if that's a way of making home.

It is a blustery day in November. The winds have been whipping the trees for days. I was going to spend this month on beaches, places with warm weather. We would have browsed through ruins and iterations of painful histories. Tourist guides will speak of these ruins with something akin to pride. I will not belong there. For someone who craves to belong, this is not a pleasurable pursuit. I was going to write an essay on this trip. I'm writing an essay but it's not the essay I thought I would write.

Once upon a time, tourism had a noble goal. Thomas Cook wanted to facilitate travel for working people. He began with organizing tours to temperance gatherings; on the trip, one was entertained and fed. There *was* a purpose: he hoped travel would eliminate prejudice and bigotry. Travel can still do that.

But so much of travel continues to promote discrimination and segregation. Is tourism good for the planet and people today? I didn't feel that in Venice. I've heard how strips of resorts and all-inclusives rip out the heart of communities. I've heard stories of locals not having access to their beaches. These deprive people who belong there from *their* belonging, from enjoying the beauty and peace *of their* land. It's packaged and sold to tourists instead. If travel is a way of rewiring your brain and understanding you are not the centre of the universe, how does the tourist business hamper that?

Airbnb began as an air mattress in a spare room: people connecting with people. Then, it became a platform turned mining industry for returns on investments. I do not need to go somewhere else for that. We have plenty of it right here. Lisbon is working on curbing the housing problem that over-tourism has brought to their city. Sixty percent of their housing has been estimated to have turned to short-term rentals. Venice is trying to figure out how to limit the excess of tourists. Locals not only cannot afford to live in their cities anymore but also more and more feel like strangers in their own cities. Local culture is gradually replaced with amenities that cater to tourists. This is a global problem. Why turn every part of the world into every other part of the world? This makes *elsewhere* less and less of that *somewhere else*. Would you want that in your neighbourhood? I don't. That is part of the fight we are fighting. Friends are discouraged when they see these developments but have a hard time talking about it. Challenging a narrative is also a trip through uncharted waters. *What's the purpose of your trip?* Whose business is it? Whose pleasure?

Buffered by unnecessary and mind-numbing luxury, cruises and all-inclusives actively prevent us from the growth and adventure travel can offer. Do we need such embarrassing levels of convenience? The illusory "luxury" yields real waste. Most of my students who come back from such trips can tell me how expensive their hotel was and what car they took from the airport to the hotel but they cannot tell me what they saw out of that car or hotel window. Some didn't leave their cabin much on that cruise ship to Alaska. They were bored. My student Lanice made me laugh out loud when she said being a tourist is "an excuse to stop using your brain, like we are suddenly all incapacitated." Ultimately, this deluge of *convenience,* and the resulting amnesia, becomes very expensive and inconvenient when we calculate the real impact and cost. What will be gained is nothing compared to what we are losing. *What's the true cost of your pleasure?*

What's the moral of this story? Other than we've lost so much moral ground already? In a world where multiple war zones leave rubble and ruins in their wake, where people starve you of humanity, where predatory finance squeezes us out of vibrant neighbourhoods, turns them to tourist destinations, I preserve what anchors me, what brings meaning. If I wasn't a tourist before, I'm a lot less of a tourist now. I do not need another trinket or souvenir. I do not want to browse through another set of ruins. I do not want to contribute to any tourist occupations. Does your travel make you more alert, attentive or aware? Does it challenge your understanding?

If you are desperate to get away from your burnout life, why do you think you will find something better elsewhere. You are the key in this transaction. Your problems follow you, but in this desperation to get away, you cause problems for others. I do not need to succumb to some vision of heaven somewhere else, or in an afterlife, when I can be part of building it right here around me. I only need to walk out my door to encounter the biggest wonder in the world, without any transactions or money exchanges—people in their vibrancy, their sheer un-duplicatable uniqueness and diversity. Do you travel like a thief or a lover? Are you a pilgrim, open to the adventure and aware of the transformative power of encountering the other, or are you just looking for a spectacle, trying to get away from your life?

Clearly the person on the visa was me. Multiple voices coming at me muddled my thoughts. Something wanted to come through. Many had a way of explaining it away. But uncertainty is a constant in my life and I've learned to be patient, to wait for the answers.

What I learned for myself is that travel is not a thing I do just for pleasure. Adventure is not reserved for vacation times; it's a daily necessity and undertaking. It keeps me grounded and sane in spaces of paradox and in-betweens. My joy resides in being able to stay in one place. It amplifies my sense of deeper roots and deeper purpose and deep repose.

I want to live in a place with people who know me. I cannot bear the thought of starting from scratch again or saying another goodbye. Relationships are key to my belonging, to feeling at home. I crave to be seen and understood. A community gives me a better chance for both. I'm exhausted with narrowing and simplifications. I still have friends who introduce me as Bulgarian. Curiosity is not a luxury; it's as important as survival. How I relate to my life will follow me wherever I go. Besides, today I do not have to go far to get out of my comfort zone.

The meaning of words we think we understand shift like sand dunes under our feet. The fluffy word *tourism* today is not cozy or benign. Tourism, like our housing, has become another way of undermining and decimating communities, where people feel they belong less and less. This is beyond gentrification; it is zombification. Words get co-opted in ways we are not privy to, and by the time we catch up to them, the damage is done. We are left with the consequences of forces that have lost their moral and ethical compass. This does not seem like a bug in the system but more a feature of it. These are precursors to divisiveness and conflict where more and more of us are relegated to being aliens, homeless literally or metaphorically. Algorithms have added another force bent on reshaping and redefining me. These days, I need to spend as much time as I can away from screens to remember who I truly am.

What is the purpose of my trip? All my life, I have travelled to root myself in a place. That is both my business and pleasure. It is not the world's job to entertain me, but for me to take interest in the world. That is my challenge and my adventure. A thought that floated into sharper focus was my desire to be where people gather to build, grow and strengthen the power of community: the one thing that gives me hope both in terms of belonging and effecting social change. That, I will travel for. A community can fight back against injustices—injustices aimed precisely at decimating the power of community.

Making Yogurt Keeps My Hope Alive

I've made yogurt for over twenty-five years. At first, didn't think much of it. My mom made yogurt, bread and cheese. When my son weaned himself at nine months and wouldn't take any milk, my mom—who happened to be visiting—made yogurt and fed it to him. He took to it. Then, they left. I had to learn to make yogurt and have made it ever since. Under COVID-19, the whole business of making came into focus with a force. My son turned twenty-seven this past year. It's not an issue of survival anymore. Why do I still make yogurt?

Since the start of the pandemic, I have been overwhelmed with teaching online, learning curves and much adrenaline. After eight hours in front of a screen, I don't sound like myself, can barely string words together grammatically. My homegrown screen concussion means you have to listen to what I mean, not what I say. You know what I mean? I began to pay even more attention to things that need time and patience to make. Attention is the beginning of devotion, says the poet Mary Oliver. But our attention is constantly stolen, fragmented, mined and monetized. What happens to our devotion then?

My kids still refuse to eat store-bought yogurt. I have myself to blame for fine-tuning their tastebuds to homemade food. Junk food here and there but who will not be seduced into junk food once in a while when it's more readily available than a hot lunch at school. When I was exhausted, when the last thing I wanted was to get up early to pack a hot lunch, I tried to tempt the kids to buy lunch from the cafeteria and failed. They loved our home-cooked food a lot more. I would smile and pack a hot lunch. After all, isn't that how I was not fooled into eating food with dangerously long shelf life, or "yogurt" with unrecognizable ingredients that tasted more like custard? If you know the taste of real yogurt, or homemade food, you don't give it up easily.

My mom tells me when Danone decided to expand to the Bulgarian market, they had to learn to manufacture real yogurt. It's hard to fool a nation who invented yogurt into buying artificially fabricated custard concoctions labelled yogurt. Even the bacteria is named after the place—*lactobacillus bulgaricus*. You don't mess with such culture. Except, it's easy to mess with it. Raise a generation on un-yogurt and you can sell them anything called yogurt. Raise a generation on a fabrication or a lie and you can convince them of anything. Making yogurt gained more significance when I lived in the United States, when I was numbed into "convenience," not to mention the helplessness and fear from the Immigration and Naturalization Services. *Don't try this at home* was the motto. *Call the experts*. Making yogurt became a way of resisting. Now, we're trying all sorts of things at home.

To make yogurt, you need a starter. You need something you can trust to begin with. I always keep a few scoops from the previous yogurt. Previous success propels. For beginners, if you don't know anyone who makes yogurt, there are the freeze-dried bacteria you can get at stores that support making. (I hear they are not as good as the real thing.) Warm up the milk on medium heat. You cannot rush this. Otherwise, the milk will burn on the bottom of your pot. Use some of the warm milk to activate your starter. That gets the bacteria all excited and curious. Along the way, someone gave me a "yogurt maker." I kept the thermometer from that contraption and continued to be the yogurt maker.

They say hope is the last thing that dies. But who teaches you how to keep it alive? On purpose, like yogurt bacteria? Bombardment with bad news these days brings its own flavour of debilitating. Zombies stopped being funny when I realized we're all being turned into zombies. Of course, they want your brains. What better metaphor for the attention economy? I see it in the kids I teach. I call this effect the fried-brain syndrome. From imaginative, playful and compassionate beings, they shrink into little screen addicts, laser focussed on a single thought: more screen time. But kids love making things. What have we done to their brains? For some of my students, dreaming "big" now means having millions and a mansion or becoming YouTubers. Mostly, they are bored and don't know what to do with themselves. I ask them: *What can you make with your hands?* We read about the tiniest of creatures who can regenerate, never die, or survive droughts, freezing and radiation in space. *What are your superpowers?* I ask them.

Before large-scale production, manufacturing was a thing of the hand. *Manufactura* in Latin means "making by hand." When you manufacture things like bread, poems or yogurt, you dwell in the present. You take pride in craftsmanship. This is essential to manufacturing meaning. That gets me out of bed; that's the starter to my every day.

Sometimes, I call my parents in Bulgaria while warming the milk. I swear those times the yogurt is tastier. My parents say things like, *Those who sing do not think bad thoughts* or, *You cannot turn the sea to yogurt but what if it curdles?* The latter is a Bulgarian saying that I discovered seems to link yogurt directly to hope. They also say, *Do something nice and throw it on the trash heap.*

I was always puzzled about that one when I was a kid but now I imagine a city dump with piles of lovely things we did for each other. What a beautiful trash heap that will be. What contributions these are to the rhizome and mycelia of our communities.

But you need the right conditions first. Once the milk is the right temperature, add the bacteria and make a gentle swirl with a spoon. My mom makes a cross in the milk. I do that too. It is a ritual, a thread that connects us like a little prayer. I wrap the yogurt buckets in towels and put them in a pre-warmed oven overnight. Make sure to leave the oven light on. Seems to sustain the temperature overnight. But there are other ways.

The origin of yogurt is ancient. Central Asian herdsmen used animal stomachs to store their extra goat's milk. Some of the milk in these skins became thick and tart, was edible and did not go bad. Perhaps that's why it's so good for your digestive system; the bacteria recognize each other. There's a whole party in your gut, a reunion, a remembering.

Attending to the small things I cannot doubt, I attend to my hope. The bacteria that make yogurt are invisible but under the right conditions become visible through the work they do. Same goes for bread yeast or cheese culture. The volunteer work in my community often feels invisible and hopeless, but sooner or later you taste the good of it, feel it in the thriving and successes of the community. Our values are invisible but when we act upon them, we see the outcomes of our values in everything we do.

In *Hope in the Dark*, Rebecca Solnit says, "though hope is about the future, grounds for hope lie in the records and recollections of the past."[97] She summons the words of Walter Bruggeman, who says, "Memory produces hope in the same way that amnesia produces despair."[98] I begin to wonder what thoughts in my mind ferment hope, what thoughts nurture my delicate mental flora, fungi and fauna. Manufacturing yogurt, I manufacture hope and sanity. Besides, it's hard to feel useless if you make something useful.

Does the same go for things like love or democracy? You cannot see them but you know them by the results of the work they do. Our planet, too, thinks in bacteria, fungi, pH, mycelia, viruses, scents, tastes and sounds. To save a planet, we have to think like a planet, attend to its small processes. If you know the taste of real yogurt, or freedom or truth, you won't give it up easily. You can tell if what you are eating is yogurt, custard, chemical soup or lies.

"To hope is to give yourself to the future, and that commitment to the future makes the present inhabitable," reinforces Solnit.[99] But you cannot think about a future beyond yourself without empathy and care for others or future generations. For that, we need to remember we are a small part of a chain; we need to remember what we value, what is life giving and life sustaining. We have to leave the selfish *individual* shell that prevents us from the solidarity and culture that is required to create the conditions for a future worth fighting for. We need to become as generous as nature has been, and still is. Each of us doing our part in a whole web of relationships. Resistance after all, Rebecca Solnit says, is first and foremost "a matter of principle and a way to live, to make yourself one small republic of unconquered spirit."[100]

My husband used to say he wouldn't leave me because he was hooked on my yogurt. That was funny, until he did leave. Now he makes yogurt. See what I mean? Once you know the good of something, you replicate it wherever you go.

Acknowledgements

Thank you to the Canada Council for the Arts who supported this project with a grant in 2021 and allowed me the time to complete a number of these essays.

Thank you to the editors of the following publications who helped polish some of the essays and gave them a first home:

"What Do You Do Again?", *Queen's Quarterly* 130 (Winter 2023).

"A Sack of Salt," *UNTIL Magazine* 14, 2023.

"Market Arguments Do Not Work for Those Who Cannot Take Part in the Market," *Queen's Quarterly* 129 (Summer 2022).

"Be a Link, Not a Fragment," *Queen's Quarterly* 129 (Fall 2022).

"Turning the Kaleidoscope," *GRAIN* 48, no. 3, 2021.

A longer version of "To Neighbour or Not to Neighbour Under a City Government That Only Wakes Up from the Developer's Kiss" in *subTerrain* 89, 2021.

"Children of the Trees," *About Place Journal, Geographies of Justice* 6, no. 3, 2021.

"How Making Yogurt Keeps My Hope Alive," *Motherwell*, February 2021, and featured later in *The Week*.

"But Where Are You *Really* From?", *Queens Quarterly* 127 (Winter 2020).

"Is This an Illness or an Accident?" shortlisted for the 2019 *EVENT Magazine* Non-Fiction Contest.

An earlier version of "It Begins with Our Words" can be found in *Scientists and Poets #Resist* (Leiden, the Netherlands: Brill, 2019).

"Bringing the Roots Home," *About Place Journal* 5, no. 2, 2018.

"Stairway to Haven," *The Summer Book,* Mother Tongue Press, 2009.

About a decade ago, Mona Fertig asked me to write an essay for *The Summer Book*. It was the first essay I wrote of the sequence of essays that became this book. "Stairway to Haven" opened a space for me to see how I could speak poetically beyond poems and write about the thoughts that did not make it in my poems. I was hooked. Thank you, Mona.

I am grateful to all since then who did not dismiss my thoughts or obsessions in pursuit of the topics in this book and those who were patient with the strangest of questions. I am grateful to all the first readers of any of these essays. Thank you for the generosity of your feedback.

I thank my community in Canada for welcoming me and embracing me, for being a part of my journey in finding a place to call home and feel a sense of permanence. Even though there is a lot of uncertainty in the world right now, at the end of the day, we are here and working together on building trust and connections, on bringing a little more security and camaraderie to our homes. Many writers I know are also hard at work building more literary community around our books.

The thought of how much we are at the mercy of each other, how we shape each other, is both a terrifying thought and a blessing. It is a thought that still keeps me awake at night and circles around itself never finding a place to rest.

I thank both my wise and beautiful children for all they have taught me about myself: about how we grow and learn, how we reflect ourselves back to each other, how we hold each other, and how much we need a certain amount of autonomy and freedom to risk becoming our own selves in the world. I had the good luck and privilege to do that for myself and I hope I have been able to create the conditions for them to do the same.

Thank you to my sister and her husband, Michael, who were first readers of some of these essays. It is in their beautiful and quiet home, with a wide vista of a view, that the essays found their final order, flanked by their cats Maya and Misty.

As always, with gratitude to my parents for patiently telling and retelling some of the stories I include in the book, for reading and for catching errors I might have made in the telling. Most of all, I thank them for creating the conditions for me to become who I am. The gatherings around home-cooked food, the sitting around the table every day, the growing of our own food; I thank them for not compromising or taking shortcuts when the scenic route is needed, and for the talking and piecing together of stories. It was only in hindsight that I understood the values they lived and worked by and instilled in us. It is in hindsight that I understood the importance of being included at a very early age in family discussions, memory building and decisions we made together as an important part of the family unit, which is the first community we encounter. I thank them for making sure that no matter what our circumstance, surrounding ourselves with beauty matters.

Notes

But Where Are You *Really* From?

1 Diana Beresford-Kroeger, *To Speak for the Trees: My Life's Journey from Ancient Celtic Wisdom to a Healing Vision of the Forest* (Toronto: Random House Canada, 2019), audio book.

Is This an Illness or an Accident?

2 Margaret Ball, *Mathemagics* (Wake Forest, NC: Baen Books, 1996).

To Neighbour or Not to Neighbour Under a City Government That Only Wakes Up from the Developer's Kiss

3. Kenneth Chan, "City of Vancouver Restarts False Creek South Development Planning," *Daily Hive Urbanized,* July 12, 2024, https://dailyhive.com/vancouver/false-creek-south-comprehensive-development-plan-process-contractor.

4 Dan Fumano, "Once Derided as 'Instant Slum,' Does False Creek Now Hold Lessons for Rest of City?", *Vancouver Sun,* June 1, 2017, https://vancouversun.com/news/local-news/dan-fumano-once-derided-as-instant-slum-does-false-creek-now-hold-lessons-for-rest-of-city.

5 Elin Kelsey, *Hope Matters: Why Changing the Way We Think Is Critical to Solving the Environmental Crisis* (Vancouver, BC: Greystone Books, 2020), 32.

6 Fumano, "Once Derided as 'Instant Slum.'"

Children of the Trees

7 Beresford-Kroeger, *Our Green Heart: The Soul and Science of Forests* (Toronto: Penguin Random House Canada, 2024), audio book.

8 Gaston Bachelard, *The Poetics of Reverie: Childhood, Language, and the Cosmos,* trans. Maria Jolas (Boston: Beacon Press, 1969), 190.

9 Bachelard, 53.

10 Daniela Elza, "pinus contorta," in *the weight of dew* (Salt Spring Island: Mother Tongue Publishing, 2012), 26.

11 Aldo Leopold, *A Sand County Almanac* (New York: Ballantine Books, 1986), 168.

12 Sandee LaMotte, "This Is Your Child's Brain on Books: Scans Show Benefit of Reading vs. Screen Time," *CNN,* January 16, 2020, https://www.cnn.com/2020/01/16/health/child-brain-reading-books-wellness/index.html.

13 Aviv Weinstein and Michel Lejoyeux, "Neurobiological Mechanisms Underlying Internet Gaming Disorder," *Dialogues in Clinical Neuroscience* 22, no. 2 (2022): 113–26, 10.31887/DCNS.2020.22.2/aweinstein.

14 "Teaching Pupils Empathy Measurably Improves Their Creative Abilities, Study Finds," Faculty of Education, University of Cambridge, accessed March 17, 2025, https://news.educ.

cam.ac.uk/teaching-empathy-measurably-improves-creativity.

15 Christine Lowther, editor, *Worth More Growing: Youth Poets and Activists Pay Homage to Trees* (Qualicum Beach, BC: Caitlin Press, 2022).

16 Annie Dillard, *Pilgrim at Tinker Creek* (New York: HarperCollins Publishers, 2007), 36.

17 Martin Buber, *I and Thou,* trans. Walter Kaufmann (New York: Charles Scribner's Sons, 1970), 57.

18 Robin Wall Kimmerer, "Nature Needs a New Pronoun: To Stop the Age of Extinction, Let's Start by Ditching 'It'," *YES! Media,* March 30, 2015, https://www.yesmagazine.org/issue/together-earth/2015/03/30/alternative-grammar-a-new-language-of-kinship.

19 Elza, "to the me inside the tree inside of me," *in the weight of dew*, 79.

20 Robert Bringhurst, *The Tree of Meaning: Language, Mind and Ecology* (Kentville, NS: 2008), 145.

21 Kimmerer, "Nature Needs a New Pronoun."

22 Robert Macfarlane, *The Lost Words,* illustrated by Jackie Morris (Toronto: House of Anansi, 2018).

23 Kimmerer and Monique Gray Smith, *Braiding Sweetgrass for Young Adults: Indigenous Wisdom, Scientific Knowledge, and the Teachings of Plants* (Minneapolis, MN: Zest Books, 2022).

24 Buber, *I and Thou,* 57.

25 Anne Lamott, *Bird by Bird: Some Instructions on Writing and Life* (New York: Anchor Books, 1995), 236.

26 Henryk Skolimowski, *The Participatory Mind: A New Theory*

of Knowledge and of the Universe (New York: Penguin Books, 1994), xiii.

27 Tim Lilburn, "Listening with Courtesy: A Conversation with Tim Lilburn," interview by Darryl Whetter, *Studies in Canadian Literature,* vol. 22, no. 1 (1997), 135–44, https://journals.lib.unb.ca/index.php/scl/article/view/8262/9324.

28 *Diminishing Returns: Creative Culture at Risk,* the Writer's Union of Canada, 2018, https://writersunion.ca/news/author-incomes-steep-decline.

29 Iglika Ivanova and Kendra Strauss, "Opinion: Precarious Work Is an Urgent Problem for Thousands of BC Workers," *Vancouver Sun,* April 13, 2023, https://vancouversun.com/opinion/op-ed/opinion-precarious-work-is-an-urgent-problem-for-thousands-of-b-c-workers.

30 Zak Vescera, "'How Did We Become an Underclass in the University?'", *The Tyee,* October 9, 2023, https://thetyee.ca/News/2023/10/09/SFU-Striking-Teachers/.

31 M-129, *Funding for the Arts,* 1st sess., 44th Parliament, 2024, https://www.ourcommons.ca/members/en/110476/motions/13197593.

Bringing the Roots Home

32 Kahlil Gibran, *Sand and Foam* (New York: Alfred A. Knopf, 1926; Project Gutenberg, 2005), https://gutenberg.net.au/ebooks05/0500611h.html.

33 Timothy Snyder, "On Freedom: Timothy Snyder with The Current's Matt Galloway," interview by Matt Galloway, *Vancouver Writers Fest*, October 27, 2024, Granville Island Stage.

34 Snyder, interview.

35 Hermann Hesse, *Wandering: Notes and Sketches* (New York: Farrar, Straus and Giroux, 1972), quoted in "Hermann Hesse on What Trees Teach Us About Belonging and Life," Maria Popova, *The Marginalian*, accessed March 21, 2025, https://www.themarginalian.org/2012/09/21/hermann-hesse-trees/.

36 Beresford-Kroeger, *To Speak for the Trees* and *Our Green Heart*.

37 Snyder, interview.

38 Seth Bunev, *Screenfarers: Nurturing Deliberate Action in a Digital World* (Cladonia Press, 2021).

He Loves Me, *He* Loves Me Not: In the Murky Waters of Online Dating

39 Aziz Ansari, *Modern Romance* (New York: Penguin Random House, 2016).

40 Thomas Lewis, Fari Amini and Richard Lannon, *A General Theory of Love* (Toronto: Penguin Random House Canada, 2001), 33.

41 Ansari, *Modern Romance*.

42 Lisa Appignanesi, *All About Love: Anatomy of an Unruly Emotion* (New York: W.W. Norton & Co, 2011), 193.

43 Appignanesi, *All About Love*, 107–108.

Market Arguments Do Not Work for Those Who Cannot Take Part in the Market

44 J. David Hulchanski, *Canada's Dual Housing Policy: Assisting Owners, Neglecting Renters* (Toronto: Centre for Urban and

Community Studies, University of Toronto, 2007), 1, https://www.readthemaple.com/content/files/pdfs/researchbulletins/cucsrb38hulchanski.pdf.

45 Elza, "An Open Letter to Vancouver's Mayor and City Council Over Co-op Lease Renewals, *Georgia Straight*, July 7, 2021, https://www.straight.com/news/daniela-elza-an-open-letter-to-vancouvers-mayor-and-city-council-over-co-op-lease-renewals.

46 Elza, "Yet Another Housing Survey, for a City That Seems to Love Them," *The Tyee*, March 19, 2021, https://thetyee.ca/Opinion/2021/03/19/Yet-Another-Housing-Survey/.

47 Fumano, "Once Derided as 'Instant Slum.'"

48 "False Creek South Provisional Vision Statement and Guiding Planning Principles," City of Vancouver, accessed March 18, 2025, https://guidelines.vancouver.ca/policy-false-creek-south-provisional.pdf.

49 Sean Antrim, "Whose Village?: A Brief History of the Olympic Village Development," *The Mainlander*, June 1, 2011, https://themainlander.com/2011/06/01/whos-village-a-brief-history-of-the-olympic-village-development/.

50 Marc Lee, "How to Build Affordable Rental Housing in Vancouver," Canadian Centre for Policy Alternatives, March 16, 2021, https://www.policyalternatives.ca/wp-content/uploads/attachments/ccpa-bc_Affordable-Housing-March2021_report.pdf.

51 James Baldwin, *No Name in the Street* (New York: Vintage, 2007).

52 Amy Fleming, "The Importance of Urban Forests: Why

Money Really Does Grow on Trees," *The Guardian,* October 12, 2016, https://www.theguardian.com/cities/2016/oct/12/importance-urban-forests-money-grow-trees.

53 Fleming, "The Importance of Urban Forests."

54 Rebecca Solnit, *A Paradise Built in Hell: The Extraordinary Communities That Arise in Disaster* (New York: Penguin Books, 2010).

55 Hulchanski, *Canada's Dual Housing Policy,* 1.

56 *Push,* produced by Frederik Gertten (Malmö, Sweden: WG Film, 2020), TVO Today, accessed March 20, 2025, https://www.tvo.org/video/documentaries/push-feature-version.

57 *Push,* produced by Frederik Gertten.

58 Hulchanski, *Canada's Dual Housing Policy,* 3.

59 *Burnaby Housing Co-op Threatened by Sell-off to Private Landlords,* The Co-operative Housing Federation of BC, accessed March 21, 2025, https://www.chf.bc.ca/wp-content/uploads/2021/10/CHF-BC-statement-on-IUOE-pension-fund-co-ops-1.pdf.

60 *Push* and *PUSHBACK Talks,* produced by WG Film, podcast, https://www.buzzsprout.com/1189295.

61 "Billions in Money Laundering Increased B.C. Housing Prices, Expert Panel Finds," *BC Gov News,* May 9, 2019, https://news.gov.bc.ca/releases/2019FIN0051-000914.

62 Hulchanski, *Canada's Dual Housing Policy,* 3.

63 *CityHallWatch* (blog), "Mayor and Council: Do You Really Understand the City's Odd Approach to Developer Profits in Justifying Tower Developments?", by urbanizta, post-

ed October 15, 2021, https://cityhallwatch.wordpress.com/2021/10/15/council-do-u-Understand-developer-profits/.

64 *CityHallWatch,* "Mayor and Council."

65 Marwa Al-Sabouni, *The Battle for Home: The Vision of a Young Architect in Syria* (London: Thames & Hudson, 2016).

66 Al-Sabouni, *The Battle for Home.*

67 Al-Sabouni, *Building for Hope: Towards an Architecture of Belonging* (Thames and Hudson, 2021).

68 Elza, *SCAR/CITY* (Montreal: McGill-Queen's University Press, 2025).

69 Jane Jacobs, *The Death and Life of Great American Cities* (Vintage, 1992).

It Begins with Our Words

70 Nicole Alexander Fisher, "Trump's administration's seven banned words are an attack on science," *CNN*, December 17, 2017, https://www.cnn.com/2017/12/17/opinions/cdc-banned-words-opinion-fisher/index.html.

71 "Iranian Poet and Activist Hashem Shaabani Executed," Poetry Foundation, February 6, 2014, https://www.theguardian.com/world/2014/feb/13/iran-middleeast.

72 Patrick Wintour, "Erdogan Ends UK State Visit by Calling Jailed Journalists 'Terrorists,'" *The Guardian*, May 15, 2018, https://www.theguardian.com/world/2018/may/15/recep-tayyip-erdogan-theresa-may-uk-state-visit-jailed-journalists-terrorists.

73 "Opening Address — 2023," NobelPrize.org, Nobel Prize Outreach 2025, accessed March 20, 2025, https://www.nobelprize.org/ceremonies/opening-address-2023/.

74 *Navalny*, directed by Daniel Roher (New York City: CNN Films, 2022).

75 Andy McLaverty-Robinson, "Walter Benjamin: Fascism and Crisis An A to Z of Theory," *Ceasefire*, August 14, 2013, https://ceasefiremagazine.co.uk/walter-benjamin-fascism-crisis/.

76 Robinson, "Walter Benjamin: Fascism and Crisis."

77 Jason Stanley, "Beyond Lying: Donald Trump's Authoritarian Reality," *New York Times*, November 4, 2016, https://www.nytimes.com/2016/11/05/opinion/beyond-lying-donald-trumps-authoritarian-reality.html.

78 Karen Yourish et al., "These Words are Disappearing in the New Trump Administration," *New York Times*, March 7, 2025, https://www.nytimes.com/interactive/2025/03/07/us/trump-federal-agencies-websites-words-dei.html.

79 Arundhati Roy, *Capitalism: A Ghost Story* (Chicago: Haymarket Books, 2014).

80 Snyder, interview.

81 Felipe Fernandez-Armesto, *Truth: A History and Guide to the Perplexed* (London: Black Swan Books, 1997), 3.

82 Fernandez-Armesto, *Truth*, 3.

83 Stanley, "Beyond Lying."

84 Snyder, interview.

85 Neil Postman, *Amusing Ourselves to Death: Public Discourse in the Age of Show Business* (New York: Penguin Books, 2005).

86 Yanis Varoufakis, *Technofeudalism: What Killed Capitalism* (Brooklyn: Melville House, 2024).

87 Joseph E. Stiglitz quoted in *Push*, produced by Frederik Gert-ten.

88 Stiglitz, "Joseph E. Stiglitz — The Road to Freedom: Economics and the Good Society — with Timothy Noah," *Politics and Prose*, May 7, 2024, https://www.youtube.com/watch?v=1IqsBKnSIa0&t=420s.

89 Snyder, interview.

90 Plato, *The Republic*, translated by B. Jowett (New York: Mineola, 2000), 210.

91 Plato, *The Republic*, 210.

92 Snyder, interview.

93 Peter Meiszner, "City of Vancouver Formally Declares City Is on Unceded Aboriginal Territory," *Global News*, June 25, 2014, https://globalnews.ca/news/1416321/city-of-vancouver-formally-declares-city-is-on-unceded-aborginal-territory/#.

94 Ursula K. Le Guin, "The National Book Foundation Medalfor Distinguished Contribution to American Letters," Ursula K. Le Guin, November 19, 2014, https://www.ursulakleguin.com/nbf-medal. Copyright © 2014 Ursula K. Le Guin.

95 Varoufakis, *Technofeudalism*, 58.

What Is the Purpose of Your Trip?: Of Ghosts Past and Present

96 Valene L. Smith, preface to *Hosts and Guests: The Anthropology of Tourism*, edited by Smith (Philadelphia: University of Pennsylvania Press, 1989).

Making Yogurt Keeps My Hope Alive

97 Solnit, *Hope in the Dark: Untold Histories, Wild Possibilities* (Chicago: Haymarket Books, 2016), 19.

98 Solnit, *Hope in the Dark*, 19.

99 Solnit, *Hope in the Dark*, 4.

100 Solnit, *Hope in the Dark*, 12.

About the Author

PHOTO: ONJANA YAWNGHWE

Daniela Elza's poetry collections are *the broken boat* (2020), *the weight of dew* (2012), *milk tooth bane bone* (2013), the b*ook of it* (2011)and *slow erosions* (2020). Poems from her sixth collection *SCAR/CITY* (McGill-Queen's University Press, 2025), were longlisted for the CBC Poetry Prize. She is the recipient of the 2024 Colleen Thibaudeau Award for Outstanding Contribution to Poetry and the 2010 Pandora's Collective Citizenship Award. Daniela lives and works on the unceded territories of the xʷməθkʷəy̓əm (Musqueam), Sḵwx̱wú7mesh (Squamish) and səlilwətaɬ (Tsleil-Waututh) Nations, also known as Vancouver. When she is not writing or volunteering in her community she works as a creative writing instructor, editor and mentor. This is her debut essay collection.